Watch Me

Choose Me

Joyus Livin Publishing

www.Joyuslivin.com

Disclaimer. This is a work of creative nonfiction. The events are portrayed to the

best of the author Cami Martin's memory. While all the stories in this book are

true, some names and identifying details have been changed to protect the privacy

of the people involved. This book was written as it was remembered by the

author. The author and publisher are no way liable for any misuse of the

information.

Cover by Kaye + Co Creative Designs

Photos by Rudolph J Tolar

ISBN 978-0-578-62336-8

Watch Me Choose Me

A true story of self-discovery and transformation after a struggle of domestic abuse to finding her own JOY.

A
MEMOIR BY
CAMI MARTIN

Joyus Livin Publishing

This book is dedicated to all survivors of domestic violence. I pray this book inspires you, brings you hope and helps you in your journey no matter where you are on that journey.

ACKNOWLEDGMENTS

Don't be ashamed of your story. It will inspire others.

I want to thank all my friends and family who did not know what was happening but as things unfolded, you stood beside me and walked with me through this journey. You gave me the strength to believe in myself, figure out my way and get through it all.

I want to specifically thank a few people that played key roles in my journey.

Jennifer Gilchrest, for your advice, stories, and guidance. You helped me figure out the how, which was a huge nudge in convincing me I could overcome that obstacle and get out of my situation. Thank you for sharing your story with me. For being my friend and checking on me throughout my journey. For literally cheering me on every day. I appreciate you more than you will ever know. You helped me so much. I am so grateful to have you in my life.

Bee Smith, thank you for giving me the opportunity to speak and the opportunity to achieve my dream. By connecting with you and the BeeInspired event, I was able to fulfill my dream of becoming a speaker. Thank you for the opportunity to share my Joy with your Joy.

Debra Elzey, thank you for being there in some dark moments and seeing firsthand what I was dealing with. You helped me in so many ways, but the biggest was that day I had to get all "the stuff" out of the house. Probably fifteen boxes of pictures, clothes, and shoes that we loaded your car down with. You moved me basically. You walked up and down three flights of stairs with a bad knee way too many times to count! I appreciate you so much. You are a phenomenal person. Thank you for just being you and being there no matter what. Love you sister!

Jaime Einhorn for helping me with edits and the cluster of headaches I felt came with it. I appreciate you, your willingness to help me in the final stages and your colorful words where they were needed.

My girls, Logan and Meghan, thank you for being two of my main reasons for choosing me and for being my strength each day when I needed it during some of my darkest times. Thank you for understanding why I needed to choose me and walk this journey. Thank you for supporting me and loving me even when I wasn't sure where I was going or what was ahead. You kept me smiling. You knew and understood the reasons I finally had to leave. Thank you for understanding that I needed to go and then encouraging me to go so I could survive. I love you both so much. Thank you for always being there, never judging and always standing by my side, even if you didn't understand.

Charles, I am not sure where to start. You walked into my life and I truly believe you were put there by God. The timing I can say I definitely questioned, but I knew there was a purpose. You were heaven-sent. I can't thank you enough for all you have done for me, all that you continue to do for me, the little things and the big things. You have helped me find the me I lost years ago. You have helped me grow in so many ways, guiding me along the way. You truly are amazing. There is no other word to describe you. You are the extra to my heart, the extra in my life, and the extra I have never experienced. I am very blessed and grateful to have you in my life, blessed at having found you on my journey. You are the king I always wanted, and you make me feel like your queen. I am so excited to see what great things we will accomplish. We have bold dreams and they are coming to fruition. We are at the cusp of changing lives and inspiring others. I love you with every fiber of my being. You truly are the man of my life and my dreams.

To my friends, family and everyone else who supported me along the way in writing this book. It started as a "this will be fun" project and ended with "This is my mission" to getting it published. There were so many obstacles, including people, that tried to keep it from being finished. Thank you to all the cheerleaders that kept me going. I appreciate every single one of you.

Prologue

I was born with extra...extra height, extra smile, extra happy, and extra positivity to get me through my crazy life.
— *Cami Martin*

My story is like a lot of women out there. It is also unlike a lot of women out there. It may be hard to read; it may be hard to comprehend. You may ask, "Why didn't you leave?" You may tell yourself, "I went through the same thing." What makes my story different? I am telling it! Very few people will tell their story of Domestic Violence. They are scared. Scared of the perpetrator, scared of the shame and guilt other people will project on them. Scared no one will understand and scared someone will ask that number one question, "Why didn't you leave?"

I am telling my story because I am no longer afraid. I am not afraid of my perpetrator. I am not afraid of the shame and judgment some will want to cast upon me. I am not afraid of those who don't understand or those that will ask why I didn't leave sooner. You know how I answer that question, *"You can't escape a prison you don't know you're in."* When I figured out what I was in I started my escape plan. I was lucky. Many people aren't so lucky. They feel they are trapped. They have to stay because they have no money, no support with their kids, no job, multiple reasons. The truth is, we all need to escape from the abuse. There are ways, there are places out there for you to go. It may seem impossible, but it is possible. My story is proof.

Statistics from the YWCA show, 1 in 3 women have been victims. 2 out of 3 Americans have never talked about domestic violence with their friends. We must do more so women like me are not harmed or killed. You can do more. We all can do more. You know someone, you have seen a sign or two. Reach out to them, see what you can do to help.

Domestic violence is real. It is happening all around us. Some people get it, others do not and cast blame on the victims. I know this firsthand.

When I wrote this book, I hired an editor. Her job was to edit for grammar, for the flow of story and structure. She took it upon herself to add judging, shaming and blaming. She told me, "You could have left at any time." She felt that way because he didn't hit me. The abuse was also my fault because I let it happen. She went on further and told me my story, "Wasn't anything different from anyone else. If I was reading this as a book right now, I would throw it across the room." Her sides notes read, "blah, blah, and so what, poor you." Wow. I was astonished by what I was reading.

As I wrote the book I worried about the judgment and shame that might happen to me. I told myself not to worry, it will be okay. That judgment and shame I was afraid of deep down when the book was to be released happened to me before it ever made it to print. The first person to read this book, who didn't know me, shamed me and judged me. I was crushed. One, I wasn't expecting it. Two, I thought I had fought those demons back from inside me. I obviously hadn't. Three, she went as far as to tell me not to list her as the editor. Her clients would not like seeing her being involved with my story.

The tears came streaming down my face. I stopped after a few minutes. No! You will not let someone who clearly knows nothing about domestic abuse take this work away from you. I stopped crying and turned those tears back into passion. That moment I also turned those feelings back into power. I will not let someone take away something I have worked so hard for, to inspire other women and men in similar situations. I will take my power and I will keep my power. I am beautiful, I am powerful, and I am strong!

CONTENTS

CHAPTER 1

HOW I GOT

HERE

"You will be happy" said life, "but first I must make you strong"- Unknown

"I am Cami. It isn't short for anything. Just plain ol' Cami." I used to say that. I no longer feel plain. Then I would add, "Cami, with a C." Everyone would call me Tammy at first, even after I said, "with a C." I am very tall. I am asked daily "how tall are you?" That question is usually followed by, "Did you play basketball?"

I got so accustomed to the "how tall are you" question I would reply, "Six two and yes" knowing the next question was if I played basketball. I jokingly tell people I've been six-two since birth. It feels like it. I have not always liked my height. In fact, I hated it when I was a kid. I was almost always the tallest girl in my class, usually taller than most of the boys.

I grew up in a small town in Texas. I was a blond-haired, blue-eyed smiley girl. A giggly girl. With hopes and dreams that every little girl has. I was adopted at birth, which I always knew. It wasn't a hush-hush story; it was a *you got picked* story. I was special. That's how I felt too. I felt my whole family was special.

My dad was a pharmacist and owned the local pharmacy in a very small-town community. The pharmacy was the place to get your medicine but also make-up, candy, household products and school supplies. During every holiday throughout the year, he would have the most exciting items displayed when you walked into the store. Valentine's Day would be a huge display of heart-shaped boxes of chocolate. There would be one great big one in the center of that display I always wanted to take home. At Christmas, he had a Santa Claus that my brother was deathly afraid of. My mother would try and take pictures of us with it and he would be screaming in every one of them.

It was fun to watch the change of holidays and seasons as the year went by. I grew up in that store. I was 2 years old when he opened it. I spent many days "working" there helping his customers. I would go and deliver prescriptions with him. I would work with him on holidays when he let his employees take off. I loved that store. I loved the people that visited the store and the employees. It was a community store. Everyone knew each other in this town.

My dad would take care of everyone, even if they couldn't pay for their prescriptions at that time. I loved my dad and who he was to everyone, including me. My mom was a stay at home mom. She volunteered for many different organizations and clubs at that time. She took care of me and my younger brother. He is two years younger than me and he was adopted as well. I remember him as a white-haired little boy. He didn't like to dress up for special occasions. We played often together and got along most of the time. We definitely fought too. We were that happy family with two kids and a dog and the preverbal white picket fence.

I had a great childhood. We lived on a cul de sac. Our best friends lived across the street from us. We were always outside playing, riding bikes and being with our friends. We had some crazy toys and even animals. We had a whirly-bird, which was a 4-seater teeter-totter of sorts. All of our friends thought it was so cool. We also had pet ducks at one time. My dad got my brother and baby ducks. They were so cute! We kept them in the back yard. Their names were Ducky Ducky and Quacky Quackly. My brother and I would try and cuddle them and carry them around. These ducks were a mess! They pooped everywhere. I had to hose off the back patio daily. When they went from being darling little baby ducks to full-grown ducks, I was sad. My dad told my brother and I we had to take them to the river where all the other ducks lived. He made up a great story so we wouldn't be so sad. He told my brother and I we could go see them all the time. We could go feed them, tell them hi. We agreed and went to take them to Trinity River. We set them free. A few weeks later we went to visit them. There were so many ducks there. We were kids who believed almost anything. Of course, we had no idea where they were, but we believed we picked the right ones and we fed them.

I look back and remember those memories and think to myself what a great childhood I had. I remember being really happy. I don't remember fighting. I remember my brother hating dressing up for Easter Sunday. I remember having lemonade stands and climbing the trees in the front yard. I remember fitting in with friends, and my family. I remember feeling loved.

It all crumbled when I was in third grade. My parents got divorced. I vividly remember my dad's car piled high with clothes. They were all on hangers and crammed into the back. I could see them through the window. It was so strange. I couldn't figure out where he was going.

He tried to explain it, but it wasn't making sense. I was eight and my brother was six. Not many in our community were divorced back in those days. The strongest memory I have of that time was my mother sitting on the floor in the middle of the living room and crying. I wanted to cry too, even though I didn't understand.

We worked our way through the separation of being away from our dad. We got to see him a lot on the weekends and during the week. The new normal started. This new life as I knew it would be ok. There's one thing I've learned about life though, it changes when you don't expect it. Mine was about to change again. I look back now and believe that this was a time that changed my life so very much.

In the middle of the 5th grade we moved. My brother, my mom, and I moved from the Ft. Worth area to Tulsa, Oklahoma, five hours away. My dad wasn't coming with us. We were moving away from my dad, my friends and other family members. So far away from my life as I knew it. I can still remember this day so clearly. The night before we left, we were standing in the garage. My Dad was telling my brother and I good-bye. The car was packed. There was nothing left in the house. As we stood in that garage trying to say goodbye, we all cried. I didn't understand why we needed to move. Life was good. We'd had a system. We'd been able to see Dad every other week or more, and now, when would we get to see him? Why was this happening?

When my Dad left, I stood in the garage with tears streaming down my eyes. He was sitting in his car in tears as well. The door slowly closed, springs creaking, light fading and the garage door slamming onto the concrete. I will never forget that day.

We moved to Tulsa because my mom had met someone. When he would come to visit my mom in Ft. Worth, I never got the feeling he liked me or my brother. He seemed like a mean person. We moved to a house that we leased in Shadow Mountain, a beautiful, hilly neighborhood in Tulsa, which was very different than the flat, barren land of central Texas.

I was a tall, skinny, awkward kid who desperately needed braces for a severe overbite. Thanks to all the perms Mom had given me, my hair was so damaged that I'd had to cut it off. It was super short—think Rod Stewart in the seventies. You might call it an ugly duckling stage, but, because of my height, I was in the ugly big bird stage. Even then, I was about five-nine or taller. A foot taller than most of the other kids in the class, fitting in was impossible. All I accomplished was looking weird.

It was very hard to make friends. I wanted to blend in. I wanted to be camouflaged. I made it through the last half of the school year by focusing on summer when I would go home to Texas to see my dad, see my friends, and be normal for a little while.

Summer was wonderful. My dad lived on the lake. We waterskied, we swam, we fished. We were out on the water on the boat every day. On the weekends we got up early before "all the crazy people" came out and hit the water. Summertime was my favorite because I was home.

When August came, I begged Dad to let me stay with him. I didn't want to return to Tulsa. However, Dad loaded my brother and me in the car and off we went. One year my brother wanted to stay with my Dad and not come back to Tulsa with me. My mom let him. I was crushed! I was now completely by myself with my Mom and a man who didn't like me. I felt my brother was the lucky one, he got to escape.

When the school year started back up, my mom wanted me to attend a modeling school. This school was similar to a charm school. They would teach you how to walk, how to wear makeup correctly and how to dress. "It was to build confidence," they told me. It did the exact opposite. One of the major requirements from the modeling school was to wear make up every day. The first time I did this, it was mortifying. I didn't want to go to school with make up on. I didn't want anyone to make fun of me. My mother sent me to school anyway. As I arrived at school, all the students were in the gym for an assembly. We were all sitting on the floor in rows according to our class and grade. A classmate next to me asked, "Why are you wearing make up to school?" I was so embarrassed. I couldn't answer them. "You look stupid with all that on," she said. I wanted to crawl into a hole. I felt ridiculous. It drew attention to me. My self-esteem had started to shrink, I was feeling more and more self-conscious about myself. I was feeling hurt, betrayal, abandonment, ugly, and I was beginning to feel unwanted.

As time went on, cliques in school got more prevalent. Bullying started. I was in the eighth grade when I was bullied for the first time. I wanted so badly to be accepted. I cared so much about what others thought of me. This was something I learned from my mother. I was taught it mattered what others thought of you. What you wore, what you looked like.

It mattered so much that my mother had my ears pinned back. It was the worst pain I had ever felt even to this day. I wasn't fully knocked out and I could feel every scrape of the cartilage and every stitch being sutured to the side of my head. I was screaming so loud my mom could hear me in the waiting area. I felt my body image was awful. I felt I wasn't pretty; I felt awkward and unattractive.

I did have some friends. There were four of us. We would go to the mall, hang out and have sleepovers. I was part of their group, even though I was the one they made fun of and picked on. Yes, I was that girl they played tricks on. I was the one they were mean to and laughed at. I was the one who would fell asleep and woke up with the magic marker mustache across my face. I walked around with it on me for hours, I did not see it and did not understand why they were laughing so hard.

The self-esteem continued to drop. One day, this same group of girls decided to play a prank on me. I don't know if it was meant to be for just a day or weeks or months. But it lasted more than a day. It lasted weeks.

My friends and I would go to the mall every weekend. We would hang out at the arcade. Go get a corn dog at Hot Dog on a Stick, walk around the mall then go over and get caramel corn which was across from the arcade. No telling how many times we would walk around the mall, we covered every square inch from top to bottom. We met other kids from other schools while we were there. Exchange phone numbers and talk later when we got home. The mall was a club for kids if you really think about it.

One night, when I was about 13, the phone rang at home. My mom answered it. She said it was for me and it was a boy. "What?" I am going over in my head who I might have met recently. Who would be calling? "Hello" I said. He replied, "Hello!" He said he met me at the mall. He had gotten my name and phone number from one of my girlfriends. We talked for about forty-five minutes. It was a great conversation. I was so happy. I couldn't believe a boy had called me. I called my friends immediately. I told them all about it. They were excited for me.

He continued to call me over the next couple of weeks. Every day, he would call me after school. We would talk for a while. He would tell me things he liked about me and that he wanted to be my boyfriend. He wanted to meet me at the mall, but we never could schedule it.

I looked forward to coming home and getting that phone call from him. This was my first boyfriend; I had never had anyone interested in me before. I was so excited. My friends and I would talk about him all the time. They seemed genuinely curious, so I'd tell them everything we talked about.

One day when he called, something happened. I heard laughter, my friend's laughter in the background. I recognized the sound. I went silent. Then they all started laughing, and then I knew. There was no boy. They made him up. How could I have been so stupid? How could they have been so cruel?

It was the worst feeling ever. I didn't go to school the next day. Maybe not even the day after that. I didn't want to be their friend ever again. I was so hurt. The pain cut deep. How could I face them? How could they have humiliated me? How could I face anyone at school, everyone was going to know! I put a guard up that day. I started to learn how to keep people at arms' length. It was one of the worst moments of my life, one that would scar me for a lifetime. I will remember it forever.

I wanted to fit in. It was a need of mine to be wanted, to feel like I belonged. I am sure everyone wants to feel like they belong at some point! Through high school, I did a few things that made me stand out with the "in-crowd." During my freshman year at the age of 14, I once bought beer for classmates because I looked older than I was. That made me feel special for about a day, actually only a night.

Once when I was a junior in high school, my mom went out of town and my friends talked me into having a party. I had never thrown a party before. This would get me noticed, talked about and make me feel like I fit in. So, I had a party. The plan was to have a few people over. Well someone told their friend, then they told a friend and the next thing you know there were over 300 people at my house. The police and fire department showed up with helicopters and fire trucks. A knock at the door shut everything down. Everyone scattered, kids were running in all directions from my house down the street. As one of the last kids was leaving my friend shuts the front door and she starts describing a boy while making a swooning movement. She falls through the front glass window! She isn't hurt but I am freaking out. I reached down and grabbed her hand and told her, "You need to call your dad right now and have him bring a check to pay for the window." I called a 24-hour window repair shop and had the glass replaced that night.

The next day some neighbors stopped me as I was leaving my house. They told me that was the most excitement that had happened in the neighborhood in years. I was worried. Someone would tell on me. My mother never said a word. Years later I told her all about it. She said she knew something about it but not the full story.

That party was the talk of the school until I graduated high school. It probably would be remembered at the high school reunions. I fit in! Albeit brief, but I felt like I fit in. I did something cool to be noticed.

My parents both remarried, ironically, within a week of each other. I swear it was like a race. It was spring break. I went to my Dad's for the break and my mom went to Hawaii to get married. When I came back, she asked if I told my dad that she had gotten married. I said yes, almost laughing. I then told her, "He got married the week before you!" The expression on her face changed drastically. It went from bliss to shock. This actually made me chuckle inside, not that she was shocked but because they were in competition to see who would get married first!

The "lovely" man we moved to Tulsa for became my stepdad. He still wasn't nice; in case you were wondering. He had a way of making me feel as if I was in the way and a complete nuisance and he didn't like me. For example, one day I had gotten my car washed at a full-service car wash, where they cleaned the inside as well. He told my mother to tell me I couldn't go there to get my car washed anymore. He said it was expensive and since he didn't get his car washed there, I couldn't get my car washed there. I got mad. I had a job and I made my own money for gas and extras. He had no say on how I could wash my car. I never said anything to him about that conversation. I continued to get my car washed there, I just didn't tell them.

My life during the time consisted of, coming home from school, doing my homework and occasionally I would hang out with friends. I also went to my part time job at Express in the mall where I worked 20-30 hours a week. If I was at home, I would normally stay in my room.

His behavior towards me was unjustified. He would go for weeks without speaking to me. We would be at the dinner table, or in the living room and he would not acknowledge I was even there. The silence was hurtful. I didn't want to be around. I can remember sitting in the kitchen at the table with my stepdad directly across from me. He would talk to my mother and she would reply. I would try to start a conversation then silence. It was awkward and made me feel anxious. My mother would answer me while he would just stare at me. His stare was cold, and heartless with no emotion and anger wrote all over his face. The silence made me uncomfortable.

My senior year it got bad, really bad with him. The tension in the house was so thick. He was angry all the time and I wasn't sure why. I felt I wasn't wanted. I wasn't loved and felt hated. My self-esteem was spiraling downward even lower than before. One afternoon when I walked into the house from school, he raised his voice at me. I don't even remember what started it. I wondered why he was even talking to me.

We lived in a condominium that was three levels. I was going downstairs from the living room and kitchen area which was the middle level. We crossed paths. He mumbled something to me. I kept walking,

I didn't hear him and the way he said it wasn't audible. He then yelled. I didn't know why he was yelling. It caught me off guard. We were both standing in the stairway. I got mad and yelled right back at him. I had never done that before. "Get out of my house!" he shouted. He was serious. I was dumbfounded. I needed to what? Leave? Go where? Why?

What had I done to trigger this from him? I hollered for my mom. She was crying. He continued to yell, "This is my house, and you are no longer welcome." It didn't matter to him that I was still in high school. It didn't matter that I hadn't done anything to cause him to be mad at me. I had not given him any reason to throw me out of the house. As I told my mom, her response to me was, "I guess you have to go!" "*What?*" I had no place to go. I was in high school. I was crying. I was hurt. Nothing was making sense to me. What was I supposed to do? I left in shock. I drove to my friend Jill's house. She had already graduated and still lived at home. After I told her what happened, she and I came up with a plan. We had already planned on getting an apartment together when I graduated. It was going to be sooner rather than later. Right then we went out to look at a few places to see what we could get quickly that day.

That same afternoon I got a phone call at Jill's. It was my friend Kim who had been our next-door neighbor. "Hey! Your mom just called my house. All your stuff is in the street!" I went home and sure enough, there it all was in the street. I was cast out into the streets by my stepdad and my own mother! I loaded what I could in my car. I fought with my stepdad over my mattress and my bedroom furniture, which I'd had since I was little. He wasn't going to let me have those things, just my clothes. I took my bed and furniture anyway, they were mine.

While Jill and I were looking for apartments, we found a leasing manager who felt sorry for me and my situation. He gave me the keys to our place. My dad had wired me money so that I had the money for a place to live. As I sat on the floor of my empty apartment, I cried while thinking, "How was I going to get through this?" I had nothing. I needed to buy food, household goods. It was three-thirty in the morning, so I went to the grocery store to find food, utensils and cleaning supplies.

This was a dark place and a dark time. A time in my life where I felt extremely alone and unwanted. Unloved, I was nothing. Numb! I was in a downward spiral of depression. Little did I know it could get worse.

CHAPTER 2

PERFECT

PREY

If you want to know what it's like to survive hell and still come out shining brighter than the sun, just look into the eyes of a woman who has survived intense damage and refused to allow it to destroy her softness, or her soul. - Unknown

I was an eighteen-year-old with no self-confidence, with no self-love, fear of abandonment, fear of losing people, and fear of being hurt by others. I was just wanting someone to love me and care for me. I just wanted to feel wanted.

Jill and I became roommates. We went out on the weekends and sometimes during the week. One Tuesday night when I was still in high school, we went to a dance club in Tulsa. You only had to be 18 to get in and my friend Jill made me go. She knew I needed to get out! It was a busy night. I had been to this place many times over the previous five months. I would always dance with my friends. I was rarely asked to dance by a guy. But on that night, I was asked twice!

The first guy asked me to dance and asked me my name. We danced to one song. The second guy who asked me to dance said he sent his friend to ask me to dance because he wanted to know my name. As we were two stepping across the dance floor, he said, "So your name is Tammy?' Over the music, I yelled, "No, it's Cami. Cami with a C."

We danced a few more times, talked and then decided to meet there again later that week. I thought we had a great night. I gave him my phone number. I was so excited someone was interested in me!

We met that following Friday night and then again on Saturday. By Saturday night, I wasn't sure I liked him. He seemed fun Friday night, but I wasn't feeling the same way the next night. I couldn't pinpoint why, but I wanted to get away from him. I tried to ditch him by hiding int the bathroom. He waited for me outside the bathroom door. I tried to hide by blending in with the other women walking out the door. He saw me trying to leave. He got mad. I told him I was leaving as I started toward to my car in the parking lot.

He followed me to my car which shocked me. Why was he doing this? As I was walking to my car and he started yelling, "Where are you going? You didn't drive here. Why are you trying to ditch me?" We were standing outside my car now. He is standing on the other side when he realized it was my car. Still yelling at me he says, "I didn't know you drove. When did you get your car here?" I explained, I had met Jill here earlier and dropped off my car. As he continued to argue with me, it became stupid. I hardly knew this guy. Why is he yelling? I started laughing, which made him start to laugh and stop yelling. That was our first fight. After we stopped laughing, he asked if we could go out on a date, a real date, a pick-you-up date. So, we made plans for our first date.

He picked me up in his car. I had never seen his car. It was a 1972 Ford Gran Torino. It was green. It wasn't a bad car. He took great care of it. I just didn't expect a classic type of car. I made a comment about his car and he took it wrong, then he replied, "You're not dating me for my car."

It was a normal dinner date, but for me, I was just happy that someone showed interest in me. We continued dating. It felt good to have a boyfriend that was real. I thought I had met the man of my dreams. I was falling for this guy. We would talk every day. He would buy me stuffed animals for Valentine's Day, St. Patrick's Day, for whatever reason he would bring me one. He came to see me every weekend during the school year. He went to college about forty-five minutes away. He would pick me up for dates and I would be so nervous. My entire body would shake. I couldn't keep my legs from shaking sometimes. He made me so nervous.

Eventually, I asked him to go to prom with me. I was afraid he was going to say no. He was in college why would he want to go to the prom, I thought. I was so happy when he said yes. I have a prom date. I wouldn't have gone without a date.

I rented a limo and we went with two friends of mine. We went out to dinner at a fancy restaurant in Tulsa. We drove around in the limo before we arrived at the Prom. Everyone drank in the limo, but he got very drunk. We walked into the hotel where the Prom was being held. When we walked in, you could get your picture taken. We didn't stop, I wanted to but he didn't. We walked into the ballroom. There were balloons and decorations.

Everyone was there, tons of people groups. I wanted to dance. We didn't dance, in fact, we didn't stay but what seemed like a few minutes. We stayed long enough to walk in, see what it looked like and walk out. None of which is what I dreamed my Prom would be like. I didn't say anything. I wanted to stay longer. He wanted to leave. He didn't know anyone, he wanted to ride around in the limo and drink. So, we left to go get in the limo. I was happy he went with me so when he said he wanted to go, I said ok. We left my friends there while he and I drove around in the limo. When we got back to my apartment, he is stumbling drunk. I had to take off his tux. At first, it was kind of funny, but that slowly faded as I realized I couldn't get him undressed. I left him passed out on the bed and went to the couch to sleep for the night.

The next morning, I was ok, I didn't want to tell him or talk about the Prom. The night was frustrating, but I had started putting all my wants to the side, I just had not realized it yet at the time. I didn't want to make him upset. This was becoming my new normal. Then something changed at about the four-month mark.

He had a summer job in Stillwater. I would go to see him on the weekends and some weeknights after work. One night during the week, I went over to see him and I could tell that something was wrong. He was unhappy, almost angry. I asked him why he was upset. He told me it was me. He told me he didn't like how I acted, how I was, then he told me I needed to change, and I needed to go home. He didn't like me. I needed to think about how I acted. He said I acted like a child.

I pouted if I didn't get my way. I acted like a brat. All my behaviors were bad according to him.

He told me I needed to leave. I needed to leave now! He said, I needed to grow up, I needed to think about what I needed to change about myself and when he was ready to see me again, he would call me. I could come back then, after that we might be able to get back together.

My entire world just crashed in on me and turned upside down. I cried all the way home. I cried at work, I cried every day thinking that the only guy in the world who liked me, suddenly didn't like me. I had such low self-esteem that I thought my life and my world had ended. I couldn't stop thinking there would be no one else that would ever like me, much less love me.

Then, out of the blue, a week later, he called me. He said I could come back and we could work on it. I went to see him. I told him I would do what was I could to change. I asked him, "How did you want me to act? Tell me, I will do it." I morphed into the person he wanted me to be. I stopped being me. It was a slow process of losing myself. I basically became a shell of myself and became a person I didn't know, someone he would like. I became the girl with no opinion. I became the girl who didn't question things. I became the yes girl.

This was a red flag that I didn't understand or see. It was so gradual that I didn't see the changes happening. I was getting into a relationship that would have many red flags, but none of which I saw initially. At this point, I should have said goodbye. I shouldn't have changed for any man or surrendered to the fear.

We continued to date and then moved in together. I thought I was living the dream. On our six-month anniversary, I found out he had bought me a promise ring! I couldn't wait to receive it. I really thought he would give me that night. I didn't get it. I was so disappointed. He knew I thought he would give it to me then. He took pleasure in the disappointment. *Another red flag.* On our one-year anniversary, he gave me the ring.

As time moved forward, we would talk about marriage often. One day we decided to go to the mall. While we were there, we looked at rings at multiple jewelry stores. It was fun and exciting. We talked more and more about getting married. Girls dreamed about this magical moment, the proposal, the ring, the engagement. Looking back at this moment it should have been a red flag as well. We found his ring first. It had eight diamonds. I thought it was a little flashy for a guy, but it was what he wanted, so I got a credit card and paid for it. We found my ring a few weeks later. It was a setting without the main stone. It was made for a marquise shaped diamond. It was very pretty which made me super excited. We opt for a Cubic Zirconia instead of a diamond. I didn't mind, it was a beautiful ring regardless. He told me he would change it out later. I really didn't care. I was in love with the ring. We left it at the jeweler so they could get it set and sized.

I kept thinking at some point he is going to ask me to marry him. I had thought of all kinds of scenarios. How would he propose? How exciting it was going to be, to be asked to be his wife. Again, the fairytale stuff we have pictured in our minds throughout our teenage years. Then reality sets in, he never proposes. I didn't get the fairytale proposal I had in my mind, none of those scenarios. He never asked me. He just tossed the ring at me and said here.

I was sitting in a recliner chair at home watching TV when he came into the apartment. He had the box in his hand, and he tossed it at me and says, "Here!" That is all he said. "You know you should ask me, not throw it at me", I said sadly to him. Then he states, "You know we are getting married, so why should I have to ask you?"

That was another red flag that I didn't notice. As I told people of our engagement, it became even more embarrassing having to answer the question, "How did he propose?" Whenever the question was presented to me, I would usually redirect the topic to anything else. I continued to do things as he wanted for the next year.

I planned the wedding and bought a beautiful dress. Found a florist with beautiful arrangements. I enjoyed the planning part wholeheartedly. I loved it so much I went to work part time at the store where I bought my wedding dress! The day finally arrived; everything was beautiful. It was held in Sharp Chapel at the University of Tulsa. Neither one of us had a church home so this was perfect.

My bouquet was amazing. It had white roses with gardenias. It flowed down towards my feet. My dress was long sleeve and had pearls and crystals all over the front. I felt beautiful.

The bridal party was upstairs getting ready while trying to keep me calm. I was so nervous. When it was time to go downstairs, the first person I saw was my Dad. I immediately started to cry. He tried to calm me down. He asked, "Are you happy?" "Yes, I think so," I said. He then told me a story I had never heard. He told me when I was a little girl, he and his friend Keith were in the front yard watching me run around. I was running around with a stick in my hand. He told me to stop because I was going to poke my eye out and be a one-eyed girl. When he had gotten to the punch line of that story I immediately started laughing. He did it, he got me to stop crying.

The funniest part of that day was when the minister said, "You may now kiss the bride." I had a veil over my face. He couldn't lift the veil over my head. His arms were too short to go over my head. I had to bend down. The entire congregation laughed.

The reception was amazing as well. It wasn't the food, drink or cake that made it amazing. We didn't get to have any of that. It was all the family and friends. Family from out of state, all my coworkers. We all danced the night away. It was after midnight when it all ended.

Our honeymoon was in Branson, Missouri. I wanted to go to the beach somewhere. It didn't need to be in Mexico. Galveston would have worked too. He didn't want to go there. He didn't like water. He didn't want to spend money on that. He didn't want to go anywhere. I finally talked him into Branson. It wasn't far and it wasn't expensive. I made the best of it and made it great. We went to Silver Dollar City, a ferry boat ride and Fantastic Caverns. We spent a few days there then we came home.

After a couple of years of our marriage, we moved to Oklahoma City. We both had great career opportunities there. I thought life was going well. We wanted to buy a house. I had gotten myself into some credit card debt before we were married, it started with the purchase of his ring. I missed some payments then wound up having to get some credit help.

He got mad when he found out. He started yelling at me. The credit help had gotten my debt paid off, but it left a mark on my credit report. We were unable to buy a house that year because of my bad credit. He made me feel so ashamed and guilty. His words were so degrading. He told me, "You can't take care of money. It is your fault we are not able to get a house." He then told me, "I lived with something similar when I was younger and I am not doing it again. You need to get your shit together." I was miserable. How could I have messed up and done this? We will never get a house now. He would never stop saying, "It's your fault!"

At that time, we had separate bank accounts. At some point after that we merged them. He kept a general ledger on each of us. How much each of us had. He made about $40,000 more a year than I did. We split the bills, half on the house payment, half of electricity, etc. I made my car payment also. I never had any money. Based on his calculations, I never made enough money according to his ledgers. If we didn't have enough money to pay the bills, it was my fault. I spent too much. I was always in the negative by how he figured the bills. It wasn't ever that we needed to spend less. He told me I needed to find another job or find a way to get some money.

For the next 20 years, all I heard was you have no money. You need to find another job or figure it out. I was always in debt with him. Did you read that clearly? I owed him. He was keeping me afloat and I should be indebted to him. He always had money to buy what he wanted. I never bought anything or could buy anything. This turned into a pattern, one I didn't even notice.

Money started to make me cower, it became an instant trigger that gave me anxiety. Talking about our finances made me sick to my stomach. It would turn into a fight that I didn't want to be in. Talking about finances made me want to crawl in a hole.

A few years later, we finally found a mortgage company that would work with us. We built a house in a small town outside of the city. It was a cute house. A few months later a shop was added that was brick and matched the house. All the extra stuff he wanted, he got. Where might all that money come from that paid for all the extra stuff? I got it for him, from my dad.

It was our first spring after living in our house for about four months, I looked forward to having a backyard full of flowers, green grass and beautiful landscaping. We were on an acre of land with lots of trees and grass. Earlier in the year, we had laid down 22 pallets of sod and I was looking forward to planting flowers and landscaping the rest of the yard.

New house, new yard, I am living the dream of being married, being the wife. The fairytale some girls grew up thinking about, cooking, cleaning and enjoying all the so called "wife" things. On this particular morning, I was cleaning the house. I had been wiping down the countertops in the master bathroom. I heard the lawnmower so I walked into the living room and glanced outside where I could see him mowing. He had an old riding lawn mower that his dad had given him. As I briefly watched him, he turned the steering wheel of the mower and it came completely off. I started laughing immediately. It was hilarious.

He could not hear me or see me while I watched him from the window. He started to lose his temper. He threw the steering wheel across the yard like a frisbee. I panicked. I had seen this anger a time or two before. He started to briskly walk inside the house. I ran back to the bathroom and pretended like I saw nothing.

I remember it like it was yesterday. I had just finished wiping off the sink areas from hairspray, my hair and the white toothpaste residue in the sink. He barged into the bathroom with an angry voice. "What are you doing?" I was acting super happy and I responded with "cleaning the bathroom." I was all smiles. I didn't want him to know I saw the whole thing. I started to walk out of the bathroom towards the living room and he stopped me. He yelled angrily, "You have missed a spot." I turn around to see what he was talking about. There was one lone hair on the counter. He was pointing out that I had missed cleaning that area. He told me, "If you are going to do it then do it right." I got mad. Actually, I'm not sure if I was mad or hurt.

He had come inside to make me upset because he was mad at the lawnmower. He succeeded. I was upset. Why would he want to ruin my day, my time cleaning, my happiness? This should have been a red flag. It wasn't. Slowly he was doing things to me that I didn't see happening. This was the start of a pattern. If he got mad, he in turn made me upset to make himself feel better. If he had a bad day at work, he would bring it home and somehow make it my fault. Slowly he was manipulating me. It happened so slowly that I wasn't even seeing it.

In 1998, we had our first baby, a girl we named Logan. She was a beautiful baby. She was a horrible sleeper and a horrible eater. This child caused me to have worry lines and premature grey hair. She did not sleep through the night until she was 6 years old. She hated food that a normal toddler would like, peanut butter and jelly sandwiches, chicken nuggets, and spaghetti. She was having none of it. She ate taquitos for months She was a bossy, speak her mind, sassy little girl. I loved every ounce of her. She was a mess! But a very loved mess.

Six years later, Miss Meghan was born. On our last ultrasound for her, we would find out if she was a girl or a boy. "It's a girl!!!!" we were told. "Great. I have 2 weddings I have to pay for now." Those were literally the first words out of his mouth. Meghan was perfect. She was the sweetest child. She slept great, she ate great, she was always happy. She was adorable!

When she did something wrong she would stop, look up at me with those big beautiful blue eyes and say, "I'm sorry Momma." How do you scold that! So she never got in trouble.

I had envisioned my house to be the house that all the kids came to. I wanted my girls to have that place, sleepovers, laughter, play dates and fun times. I wanted our home to be a safe place for everyone. That wasn't how it was at all though. They rarely got to have friends come to the house or have friends spend the night. He didn't want anyone to come over. The girls would ask to have someone spend the night, his answer was always, "What for?" He would always say this in a gruff tone, as if having someone over was a bad thing. I felt bad for them. I would hush them many times so they wouldn't make him mad or angrier. It wasn't worth his wrath when they would ask the question, "Why?"

The days started to take on a similarity. I took the girls to school and daycare. I would go to work, do my job during the day and he would go to work to do his job. I would pick up the kids from daycare and school. We were living a normal life on the outside. It was inside the house that wasn't normal. I was not seeing the patterns that he was doing. I was oblivious to it all. I should have noticed how he was speaking down to me. He told me I was so selfish. The most selfish person he knew. He would say, "You are a bad cook, you don't know how to cook anything right." He would also say, "You are a bad cleaner, you are bad at cleaning our house." He would say this about everything I did. It would hurt my feelings and make me sad and angry. It was humiliating and degrading to me. It made me not want to cook or clean or do anything. He would boast than on how he does everything and does it very well. All this is said in front of the girls. He had them believing it so deeply that they went as far as telling me I was not a good cook. The girls would begin to mimic some of the things they heard over and over from him. This was also a blow to my self-confidence that I wasn't a good mom or wife. It would make me feel sad and inadequate.

When he had a bad day, it was taken out on us, it somehow turned into our fault. He yelled at the slightest things and put me in a place that I wanted to run from. I wanted to freeze up and shut down. It had happened at such a slow pace that it became the norm, one of which I didn't see happening as time passed. On a bad day, if he walked into the house and he saw clutter on the counter, he would yell. If the girls left something on the floor, he would yell. If he got mad and they were near him, he would thump them on the head, hard. If he walked by them yelling, they would flinch because they knew they were about to get thumped on the head. This happened regularly.

It was the girl's job to bring the empty trash cans back to the house. One time he came home and they had not brought the cans back up from the curb. He came inside the house after work and immediately started yelling, "No one listens to me in this house! No one does anything I tell them to do!" His anger and his yelling would make us all scared. He would yell and scream so loud that the venom in his voice would cause me to shut down and want to flee. The girls would start crying. My anxiety would go through the roof.

I am losing myself along the way in this fairytale land I thought I was getting. My identity, all my choices, all my desires, all my wants and dreams were slowly fading away. Is this what a marriage is? It started very slowly. I didn't even see it happening. What I also didn't see in myself, was my willingness to give, to please, to fix it at all cost. I was a giver. I was a pleaser and he was a taker. When you blend the two, I lost on both fronts. I was going to do what he wanted to make sure he was enjoying himself despite if it was something I wanted to do or not. I didn't notice that I was no longer getting a choice. I didn't notice that he didn't care what I wanted to do or what thoughts I had about anything. It was only him, his things and what made him happy. What he believed in, what he liked and if I didn't like it, tough. If I had another opinion, then I was wrong and berated for having that opinion. I stopped having an opinion. I stopped wanting to do for me. There was no compromise on his part. There was only a raised voice and me shutting down.

If you talked politics with him, he would instantly be infuriated if your opinion didn't match his. He started listening to Rush Limbaugh on the way home from work. By the time he got home he was so heated, I would have to leave the room or the house. I came up with reasons to go to the grocery store or anywhere else.

When I didn't want to do his things or if I disagree with what he thought or believed, then he informed me I was wrong. The name calling began again, he shouted at me saying "I was the most selfish person in the whole world." In that same breath, he said, "You never have an opinion on things, you never speak up and you never say what you think!" Why would I speak up? Why would I want to? He made it to where I felt I couldn't. I would be ridiculed and shamed for having an opinion. *Let me restate that, for having an opinion, I would be ridiculed and shamed.* He really only wanted me to tell him my opinion when it was in agreement with his, and when it was not, I was belittled.

This was my life! I walked on eggshells when he was around. I knew I was going to make him mad every day. It didn't matter what it was. I knew at some point that day I was going to be yelled at, told I couldn't do it or I wasn't good at it. He would yell, "You are a terrible mom!"

I was a terrible mom because I allowed Logan to go see her friends during the week or gave her permission to spend the night at a friend's house on the weekends. "She should stay home, why can't you stay home?" he would exclaim.

During the softball season, Logan and I were going to practices which meant we were gone for hours. His words rang out over and over again, "You are always keeping the road hot. You can't stay home for more than five minutes and you are teaching her the same thing!"

Cleaning, cooking, driving, parenting, laundry, my job, having friends, you name it, I was bad at it. My body, my exercise, my clothes, my height, my feet, my teeth, my smile, my eyes, my ass and my boobs were all items he used to demean and humiliate me every day. When I would come home from work, the gym or somewhere with the girls, he would tell me, "So you finally decided to come home." That statement made me not want to come home at all. I would work out longer and longer each day at the gym. I would go to after hour work events. I would do whatever I needed to do to stay away.

I got to a point where I couldn't figure out what was making him so unhappy. I am a pleaser, a fixer and I wanted to fix whatever was wrong. Whatever I was doing that wasn't working, I wanted to change to make things better. So, I started making changes. I started doing things that I normally wouldn't do or even consider agreeing to do.

As I mentioned earlier, he humiliated me about the many parts of my body. My breasts were a daily source of conversation. He talked about me having a breast augmentation for many years. I was excited over having bigger breasts. We went to the plastic surgeon for a consultation. The size was discussed by all. I tried on different implants in my bra. I wanted a full D. I would have been excited over that size. He was not going to allow just a full D. If I was doing this then it was going to be at least a DDD. He told me if I didn't get that size, "Then I was not getting a boob job at all."

I had the surgery and got extremely large implants. It was very hard to find tops that didn't make me look so big. I would buy bigger clothes, less revealing so that my chest wouldn't seem so large. When I would buy clothes, I found I was not a DDD, I was actually a 36 G. A few years later he didn't like them, they needed to be even bigger. He tried to get me to make them even larger. We went to multiple plastic surgeon's offices who looked at him like he had lost his mind. No one would agree to do it. I had not planned on going through with another surgery, I was just going through the motions to appease him at this point. The doctors were truly appalled at what he was asking.

That was another example of how I couldn't make him happy. No matter what I tried, or tried to do differently, it didn't work. There was no 50/50. There was no meeting in the middle or compromising. I didn't mind get larger breasts, but not the *giant* size that I *had* to get in an attempt to please his wants.

It was 2015 and I couldn't take much more. What is it that I can do to fix our marriage? He had mentioned divorce a few months back. I wanted to make our marriage work. I didn't want to get divorced. I didn't want to give up. I wanted to fix whatever it was causing the problem. That is exactly what I told him too. "What can I do to make our marriage work? What can I do to make you happy?" His response was to fulfill a fantasy he had. We had talked about it many times before but it was never an option that I "ever" considered. It was one he had asked me to do many times over the year and I said no. He wanted it so bad that he would say, "Tell me that fantasy that you will never ever do." He would ask me to tell him the story during sex, or whenever he wanted to get aroused. This got him excited. I would have to repeat all the details of this elaborate fictitious story that he dreamed up. I knew I couldn't do it. I didn't want to do it. "No!" I would say, "Why would you want me to do that?" Many times, I said no. Then my thoughts started questioning. I thought, what if it would make things better? What if it would finally make him happy? What if it would make our marriage solid again. If I could do this, then I could fix it. I felt I needed to fix it, I told myself.

CHAPTER 3

Sex, Lies and Videos

She's been through hell and came out an angel. You didn't break her, darling. You don't own that kind of power. – BMM Poetry

What did he want? What was his fantasy you might be asking? He wanted me to have sex with other men so he could watch. He wanted to take pictures of it, video it. He wanted to replay it later for his enjoyment. I didn't want to do it! But I felt that, if I did it, it would fix things.

I remember he had been out of town riding motorcycles with his buddies. He was texting me, telling me his fantasy. He explained how it would go down and how hot it would be. So, when he came home from his trip, I finally said ok. If this was what he really wanted and if it would make things better with us, then I would do it. He was so excited he couldn't believe it. He was so happy that I finally agreed, although I would have phrased it as "gave in" or "felt I had no other choice."

He started making plans. I was trying to act excited, no matter how nervous I was, no matter how scared I was about it. I asked myself, "How does this work? What do we do?" As he started to describe how it worked in more detail, I asked him, "Is this really a thing?" "Yes, it is a thing," he said. "Oh wow," I replied, "How is this a thing? I need you to explain all this to me." I wanted to know how it worked, what it all meant, how we would approach people, where would we find people? Had he already thought all these things out? Yes, he had.

He answered all my questions. It was called a "Lifestyle". There are many different roles in the lifestyle as well. Ours was going to be way different than I had ever imagined. His fantasy was for me to have sex with other men. He wanted me to be his Hot Wife. That was the name of this lifestyle.

A hotwife was someone who has sex with other men while their husband watched. Some men in this lifestyle are considered Cuckolds. They like to be submissive to their wives and have their wives speak in degrading ways to them. Tell them they are worthless to have sex with and could never compete with other men. He wanted to be a cuck, he wanted me to degrade him and to be mean to him after the sexual encounters with other men. But I could not talk to him or anyone in that way. I also couldn't say humiliating, degrading things to him nor belittle him as most Hot Wife's would do. That was not my personality, that is not who I was. So, the cuckold part wasn't really a part of our lifestyle.

It was so surreal that I was actually going to go through with this. I was going to have sex with other men. I had never been with anyone other than him for 30 years and all that was about to change. The first time was about to happen and I was nervous. I was freaking out! I didn't know what to expect and I was very uncomfortable and scared. He had found someone online. We were to meet him for drinks and see if there was a connection of sorts. We met at a local restaurant and sat at a table in the bar area. We talked for a couple of hours or so. We talked about some of the normal things like you would when meeting a friend for drinks. It was an out of body experience that I kept asking myself, "Why am I doing this". He seemed like a nice guy. My husband was over the top ready to go. The guy was ready to go as well, but he was also a little nervous.

It was decided, it was a go after the couple hours of conversation. We went to a hotel room down the street from the restaurant. My husband and I checked into a room while our new friend waited in his car for us to text him to come up. I had brought a bag with us with a piece of lingerie to change into inside it. As we started to get ready, I could feel my body started to shake. I was so nervous and afraid. My heart was pounding. I wasn't sure what to expect. Was I going to be excited? Was I going to be sad? What emotions would I have? I had all these questions stirring in my head while my husband kept telling me, "This is going to be awesome. Now, this is your decision, but I would be really disappointed if we didn't go through with it. You need to do it if you want things to be better."

He texted our new friend and told him to come up to the room. We sat on the couch in the room and chit chatted. I kept thinking, "How do we move from here? What are we supposed to do?" I felt awkward and uneasy. I didn't know how this worked. I felt like I was the odd person out. I was nervous and uncomfortable. I thought my husband and this guy knew what the next step was and I didn't.

Our new friend, I will call him Tony, leaned over and kissed me. Just kissing another man was strange to me. He then took his hand and touched me on my leg. I now have a whirlwind of thoughts rushing through my head. I felt self-conscious about my body, another man is about to see me naked. He continued to kiss me on the couch. He then stood up, walked me over to the bed and took off my lingerie. I looked at my husband and he had a giant grin on his face. He was excited as he filmed me with a video camera. I was becoming more and more numb as the night progressed. I don't remember all the details of that night but I went through with his fantasy. I had sex with Tony, a man who wasn't my husband, while my husband watched. Afterward, my emotions surfaced. I felt guilt, remorse, a feeling of betrayal from him and myself. My husband enjoyed it all, a lot more than he expected. He was pleased I did it and it showed him I was committed to saving our marriage. Our new friend Tony enjoyed it and said, "I had a great time, text me next time you guys go out."

After that day, my husband started investing in special video cameras and cameras that took HD pictures. He spent a couple of thousand dollars on camera equipment and computer editing software. He would have 3 or 4 video cameras set up around the room so that he could get every angle. I didn't want to be videoed. It made me extremely uncomfortable, I told him this multiple times. He assured me it was just for him. He wanted to be able to go back and watch them over and over. He would never do anything with them he told me. They were just for him.

We met with Tony again. We would see him about once a month. Each time it got easier for me. I could see how happy it was making my husband. He liked it. He was the happiest I had seen him in years. He was showing me more affection, he was being more loving and he wanted to have sex more often with me. I felt like I was loved and wanted. The fights had almost stopped. He couldn't wait until our next rendezvous with Tony and would talk about it all the time. Yes! I did it. If this is what it was going to take, then I would continue.

He bought me sexy lingerie and erotic platform shoes. Many I liked because I felt sexy in them, but I lost that feeling when he said, "don't take your clothes off you don't look good naked, you look much better with something covering you." He started to convince me that this was true.

He became obsessed with the videos and photos. He started finding porn sites. He wanted to post the pictures on them. I was uncomfortable with it. He said he would fix it by editing the pictures so no one knows it was me. The first time I found out I panicked. I wanted to see the picture that he posted, but it was hard for me to look at myself. He showed me. It was a cropped picture. You couldn't tell. He assured me he would never post anything that showed my face. His fantasy progressed even further into something else. It went from a fantasy to looking at other men's posted pictures to posting a few pictures that he had to a complete obsession with the Hot Wife Lifestyle.

He loved being popular on these sites by getting likes and comments. He posted, commented and chatted online every day. He would post pictures of other women he would find on the internet as well. He posted hundreds of pictures of them. He found that the more pictures he posted, the more points he would get to becoming the top member of the site. He loved being the top member and getting all the accolades. He was becoming addicted to the attention. It started consuming his life. He would be online from when he got home from work until he went to bed. He would get messages from other men giving him kudos. He became the idol of every man on that site. They were in awe of him and his Hot Wife.

Tony got to be not enough for him. My husband wanted more men. He in fact, had a goal of me having many men. He wanted to keep count, like notches on a belt. He found various internet sites and groups on Facebook to meet new people. He made it my job to talk to the people on the sites and find us another guy. I would join these groups titled things like Friends with Benefits or Hot Wife groups and start conversations with everyone. I would get their contact information and we would send messages back and forth. I would "Report" back to him who I talked to that day or what new person may have messaged me.

Joining these groups was a lifeline. There were both men and women in them. It was like a club. Everyone welcomed me when I joined the club. It was a good feeling for me. I was popular. Everyone thought I was pretty, much prettier than I thought of myself. I had great conversations with them. It was not just about sex and meeting up with people. It was a community. They befriended me. It was great. I made friends where I could talk about anything. It made me feel good to able to talk to people that were not at work and didn't criticize me. It was a special group of people which include some fantastic open-minded individuals. I was the one interacting with them via messages, not my husband, he would be on the computer on the porn sites. This was slowly turning into a problem. He didn't like all the messaging. He wasn't feeling the love or attention like I was getting in the messages. People in the groups were messaging me or text me on my phone. Friends we had and hadn't even met were talking to me by various means of communication. He had to know what was said. I would let him see the messages. They were nothing but friendly exchanges. The texting got to be too much for him. He wanted to know every detail of every conversation. I had to "Check in" at the end of the day and give him my phone so he could see who I talked to and what we said. I got a lot of group messages. My phone was going off constantly. He would get mad and tell me "You are always on your phone" "I guess I need to join Facebook so I can talk to you." He would say this in front of the girls. Then they would start repeating it as time went on. I was not on my phone any more than he was on his computer. He did not see it that way. The time he spent on his computer was different. I needed to get off my phone, but I was communicating with all the people he wanted me to befriend. What was I supposed to do? The ugly mean person in him started to slowly creeping back in.

These groups of friends would get together at various "Meet n Greets" so you could see everyone face to face and really get to know each other better. I was making more new friends. I loved the Meet n Greets. We would meet at clubs and dance, have drinks and just enjoy the environment. It was fun. I liked being out and dancing. It made me excited and happy. I am a very social person and I was getting back into my element. He went a few times with me, but he would sit at a back table and watch me interact with everyone. I smiled, laughed, talked and had a great time. He didn't like it. He hated it!

The first time he went with me, I got up to go greet everyone as they came in. After one of those times, when I came back to the table to sit down, he had this look on his face, bafflement. I said, "What is wrong?" He told me, "I'm wondering where my wife is?" I didn't understand his comment. He said, "Who are you? Why are you acting like this, greeting everyone, all happy and laughing?" I stared at him with a puzzled look on my face, then I smiled and said, "I am being me; you must not recognize her." We left shortly after that statement. I was finally feeling myself. I had lost that person years ago. I was feeling happy and enjoying being around friends. Dancing, going out. It was nice. He didn't like this person. This was the person who he had changed at the beginning of our relationship. She was slowly coming back.

After about a year of our new "Lifestyle," he started to change. It started with him getting upset with the messages I was getting, then it moved on to the Meet n Greets where I was having a great time dancing. Now it was about to go to a whole other level of anger and frustration with the sex.

First, my husband, the man who begged me to give him this fantasy, started getting mad after each sexual encounter right after they would leave. "You know you don't act like that when you are with me." That then morphed into, "You sure have turned into quite the actress with these guys." I asked him, "Isn't this what you wanted? Don't you want me to look like I am enjoying it? Don't you want me to act like this for you and your camera so you can watch it later and enjoy it?" He then replied with, "It just seems like you are enjoying sex with them more than you enjoy sex with me".

In a way, I was! These men were my friends. We talked all the time, not about sex but life in general. They would tell me things about them, they would tell me I was beautiful and I was just an awesome person all around. They would also say how they would never share me with other men if I was their woman. Those things started to play in my head. All of those things started to affect me. Especially the way I was being treated by them. I started paying more attention to everything, to them, to him and to myself. What did I really want? My feelings and my thoughts were starting to shift.

When we started this lifestyle, I needed to know afterward that he was ok with what had just happened and that he enjoyed it. I needed to know that all was fine with us as a couple, for me that was him wanting and desiring me. He showed he wanted me by having sex with me after, by him telling me how much he liked it and how he was happy that I was doing it for him. All of that started to change as well. He didn't want to have sex with me afterward anymore. He wouldn't talk to me for hours afterward. He would make me feel miserable. He was either silent to me or he would huff n puff and breathe heavy. We would go eat after each encounter and he would not talk for me the whole time we were there. He would make me feel humiliated. When he finally spoke to me, he would call me a whore or a slut. I felt degraded. He would say to me, "You could at least act like you like having sex with me still." But I didn't though. I started to hate having sex with him. I started not liking to have sex period. I was pulling away from him and he could feel it.

"Let's do something different, let's have a hotel party" he said. I said yes because that meant friends and people I wanted to be around. He made me miserable, they made me happy. Yes, let's do that. We planned for the party. We had about 20 people show up. We all hung out, had drinks and told stories. I knew the night would end with me having sex with our current guy, Joe. I liked him. He was very nice to me. So, I talked it out in my head and made it ok with myself.

One thing I didn't mention earlier. We had rules in place. The rules were that I wasn't allowed to be by myself, have a door closed or cuddle with anyone after sex. The cuddle part wasn't a thing. I didn't want to cuddle with anyone. He wanted the sex act itself then he wanted them to leave immediately.

The house party night I told him to enjoy himself. I told him to do something with someone else. I had gotten to the point where I was so unhappy that I didn't want to be with him. I didn't care what he did. I didn't want to be with him because of how he was treating me. He said he didn't want to have sex with anyone, but he wouldn't mind, spanking or flogging someone with a whip if they wanted him to do it. As the night went on a couple was there and the woman desired to be whipped and spanked. He was very willing. They walked into the bedroom and the first thing he did was shut the door. In fact, he looked me straight in the eyes with a devilish smirk and then slammed the door. I couldn't believe it. It was the number one rule for me and it was the first one he broke it in a matter of seconds. After he was finished, he then went to another room then crawled into bed with a couple of women started cuddling with them and again, someone shut the door. I literally was dumbfounded. I wasn't sure if I was mad, hurt or what the feelings were that I was having. The one thing I did know was that I didn't like how he was acting because he was acting out to hurt me on purpose. That night ended with me not having to have sex with Joe or anyone.

It was now time to go home and everyone started to leave. My husband was super happy while I was between pissed and hurt. I told him to have fun with someone, that wasn't why I was upset. I was mad because these rules he had were one sided and he didn't seem to have to abide by the same set of rules. I told him what I was feeling. He didn't care. He got mad at me for saying something about it. He just knew he had fun.

My eyes were starting to open wider and wider as the weeks went by. Things were changing. I wanted out of this marriage, I wanted out of being controlled. I was seeing the control very clearly now. I no longer wanted to be the "Hot Wife." It was making me very uncomfortable. When we met with our friends, he was saying things to them that were derogatory. He started getting mean and I was growing more and more miserable.

My new lifestyle friends helped me see myself for who I was, a fun happy person. They reminded me that I enjoyed being out and being with people. I learned from them that I had a personality that was being stifled by someone who had to have control of me. I was questioning if he really loved me. I questioned it so deeply that I wondered had he ever really loved me. What he really wanted was to watch the videos and look at the pictures he took of me with other men. He only wanted to have sex with me if we talked about his fantasy the entire time that we were having sex. This wasn't a loving marriage. This wasn't someone who cared for me. It was literally killing me inside. He thought I was enjoying myself too much, when in fact I wasn't. I was a great actress on the outside but I was dying inside.

We had a conversation one night lying in bed. I told him, "I am done having sex with other men. No more. It is killing me inside. It is making me miserable and I am losing myself slowly. I have to stop." "Forever?" he asked in a panic. "Yes, forever" I said. "Why not just take a break?" he asks. "No. No breaks, I want to be done." I said. The friendships I had made had built up my self-esteem, my self-confidence. It made me think and see that my marriage was not what it had appeared to be. I was seeing it so clearly. I started to realize I was in a controlling relationship. I began to see I was married to an angry, controlling and possibly a narcissistic personality. I was learning that everything he had been blaming me for was not all my fault like he wanted me to believe.

He would never own any of the problems and certainly would never meet me in the middle to help fix what was broken with us. I no longer felt I could save this marriage. I needed to change some things and they needed to be quick changes. Call it survival or call it instinct, but all I knew was that I needed to save me. I started thinking about apartments, places to go that I could afford on my own. The financial part was difficult. I wasn't sure how much my paycheck was after taxes, how much the electric bill would be or what everything would cost. Could I afford it all on my own? What size of an apartment did I need and where would it be? I had no answers to all these questions. These were things I started thinking about daily. He really didn't understand the extent of my unhappiness, the extent of my pain or what I was feeling. He saw, felt and understood nothing. It was time for me to figure it all out, something that was way overdue. I started making a plan of what I needed to do to leave as the days went by.

I started coming home later. I went to the gym and worked out. I had been doing this for the last few months, but I stayed later and later. I didn't want to go home. A week or so later he started noticing the changes. They were that obvious. He started seeing the positivity in me drifting away and saw my smile was fading. I was moving into a very dark world. I didn't know how to survive in this world. I was one who lived in the sunshine with rose-colored glasses on.

We had been married for 26 years. We had been together for 30. I told him maybe we should separate, even if it was for just a week or two. I needed to find myself and I needed to feel better about things. I told him I needed to go away. He started to freak out. He went into a panic and fear set in. As he began to have an anxiety attack, I knew I had to be careful with how I proceeded. I needed to be smart as I planned my next steps and move slowly. I needed to make the plan for a safe escape. I would have to execute my exit plan with caution. I decided my next step was to get away for a couple of days since his panic attack was scaring me. What would he do to me or himself? So, I said, "Not to leave you, just go away for the weekend and be by myself to think. I need to get away from you, the girls and everything for a of couple days." At that moment I realized, I had never been anywhere by myself. Whenever I went somewhere either the girls were with me or he was there with me. I remember he would leave three to four times a year to ride motorcycles with the guys and to go hunting in the fall. I never had any alone time or trips. I couldn't hang out with anyone without some kind of repercussion happening. Years before when I did, he would make it so terrible for me afterward that it wasn't worth going. However, this trip was different. I wasn't asking. I told him, "I am going in 2 weeks. I don't have a plan but I will by then." I felt excited, and I felt some freedom. I started planning the trip by selecting a place, finding a route and it all was fun! It was going to be the first weekend of November. I was going to drive to Missouri. I had a Camaro so driving through the winding roads of Arkansas and Missouri sounded amazing!

I called it "My Reset Weekend." I was going to reset my brain, my thinking, my goals, my feelings and my life. "What did I want?" I thought. I wanted to find myself, see myself and figure out who I was. Make sense of what had been happening to me over the last 30 years of my life.

CHAPTER 4

OPERATION

RESET

Reset your life and fill your heart with

joy, love and happiness...

Delete the bitter experience of the past

so it cannot blackmail your present...

Live each and every moment of life and

become the writer of your own story....

Live your dream...-Unknown

I drove myself to Table Rock Lake in Branson, Missouri. It was November and the leaves were just beginning to change. I knew it was going to be a beautiful trip. It just happened to be a great time of year. Fall was my favorite season, perfect for a drive. The temperature was great. It was probably close to 70 degrees. As I drove, I felt the excitement building. I was getting energized with each mile I drove. I exited off the highway and headed towards the winding tree -lined roads of Missouri. This was the best idea ever!

While I was driving, I listened to music and I found some songs I really liked. I started making a playlist of feel-good songs. The windows were down and the sunroof was open. The sun was shining and the leaves were showing their colors of copper and red all around me. I smiled and started to feel at peace. I started feeling other sensations as well. I felt the heat of the sunshine and how it was reviving me. I started feeling happier as I listened to certain songs. I felt excited watching the leaves fall as I sped down the winding roads. I was trying my best to catch a leaf through my sunroof! It was one of the best driving experiences of my life. A few more hours of driving and I arrived at my destination.

The Chateau on the Lake was the place I picked because it overlooked Table Rock and it had a balcony. Once I arrived at my room, I dropped my bags and went to the balcony. I wanted a nice view of the lake. Oh my gosh, I never imagined the view would have been so beautiful. This location was going to be amazing. It was going to be better than I even dreamed. There was a chair and a side table on the balcony which made it perfect! I had brought my journal, my iPad and my phone to listen to my playlist.

When I arrived it was early afternoon. The sun was overhead, it wasn't too hot or too cold. I sat out on the balcony and looked out over the water. I listened to the sounds of the water and the birds. I closed my eyes and sat there for a moment. I felt the warmth of the sun shining on me. This was my first time to stop and be in the moment in a very long time. It felt good to be there. It was refreshing to have no contact with anyone and to just be by myself.

I stayed out on the balcony the entire weekend. I went out at sunrise and stayed to watch the beautiful sunset each night. I took pictures, I wrote and I listened to music. I researched quotes and found books to add to my reading list.

I started thinking about what I wanted. Some things that I had wanted to do for years and I knew I needed to just do it. I started realizing my dreams. I made goals, lists and affirmations. This trip was just what I needed.

I ordered room service all weekend. I had the best hamburger and beer the first night. It tasted as a burger had never tasted before. I felt like all my senses were heightened. I had eggs benedict for breakfast the next morning, also out on the balcony. I was out there with the sun or with the moon. It was the best thing I had ever decided to do for myself.

I had equipped myself with a plan, I knew what I wanted and what I liked. I found the things I wanted to do, I realized my dreams and what I wanted to make happen. My mind was clear for the first time in years. My heart and my head felt at peace. It was amazing. Now it was time to go home and share my excitement. I looked forward to sharing the details of my trip and my future plans.

I drove home the same way I drove there, along the winding tree-lined roads. Leaves were falling everywhere, even more than when I had come through a few days before. I wanted to catch a leaf so bad! The sun was out and it was shining through the trees. It seemed like it was following me. It was right there beside me. I wanted to close my eyes, lift my face up to it and just feel it. I cruised down the road with my windows down and the sunroof back. The engine roared from time to time. Making it a perfect drive. There I was feeling so positive, so energized, and in touch with all my emotions. The sunshine, listening to my playlist, and being lost in the moment brought a huge full-on smile. I loved the thoughts and feelings I had at that very moment. I had found my Joy. I had found a fabulous word that described my whole weekend and what I wanted my life to represent. From this point forward I wanted Joy. I wanted to give joy, feel joy and be joy. I wanted to be "Joyous." I wanted to be the person who inspires, brings happiness and light. I was choosing it from this point forward.

I pulled into the garage; I was so happy when I walked into the house, I was almost dancing. My girls heard my car pull in and they met me in the kitchen screaming, "Moms' home! Yeah!" While hugging them, I was thinking to myself, "Is he going to come to say hi? Surely so." I looked around and no he wasn't coming to greet me. He was sitting in his chair in the living room. He had never moved. "Hmm, ok," I thought as I walked into the living room. I was still smiling as I approached his chair he said to me hatefully, "So you finally decided to come home?"

I stood there, dumbfounded. My smile felt like it was ripped off my face. I lost all my joy, my happiness and my smile as everything went away. It literally took him 5 seconds to take all those feelings from the weekend away.

I walked out of the living room and I went straight to the bathroom. I decided I would take a bath and gather myself back together. We had a large jacuzzi tub. I ran the water, added bubble bath and filled it up as high as possible with as much hot water as I could stand. I brought my phone and earbuds. I wanted to listen to the playlist I had created to get myself back to that peace and joy I had just walked into the house with a few minutes ago. I needed to retrieve it. I stepped into the tub, sunk deep into the bubbles all the way up to my chin and I pressed play. Then I closed my eyes as Michael Bublé started crooning "Feeling Good" to me. "Yes!" A smile slowly crept to the corner of my lips, then grew to a perfect peaceful smile. Ahhhhhh, yes, I slipped back into my bliss and my joy.

A few minutes later he walked into the bathroom. Like a needle on an old fashion record player that had just been moved too fast across the record, my tranquility came to a screeching halt. He leaned against the vanity and said to me, "Well, tell me all about your weekend. You were so excited when you came home. So, tell me all about it." His voice was so hateful and condescending. I sat there for a minute, my natural response then was to shut down, to not speak or run away. I couldn't run away. So, I didn't do anything. I just stayed motionless in the tub.

I heard my inner voice say to me, *"Tell him."* I laughed to myself. *"Ya no. That is not happening. I'm good."* He didn't need to know anything. He didn't deserve to know what my mindset was at that point. I knew he was just going to rip my joy away again by making fun of me or telling me hateful things. I thought, *"I'm good, no thanks, I'll pass."* The voice came again, "Tell him" I tell myself in my head, *"Nooo. I am not telling him."* "Tell him!" This time it was a shout. *"Ok, ok. I will tell him, but I am doing so reluctantly."* So I proceeded to tell him all about the weekend. I told him about the drive and the leaves. I told him about the hotel, the room service and the balcony. I told him about the lake and the journaling. As I talked, I could feel all the joy and excitement come back to me. I started reliving the weekend and I got energized again. I told him my goals and dreams including the one dream that I was passionate about the most. I wanted to be an inspirational speaker. I wanted to inspire people. I told him that I knew it was something I had been called to do for years but I had been afraid to pursue. I really wanted to be a speaker, I felt it in my bones and I was going to start working on it.

He stands there for a moment, still leaned against the vanity with his arms folded. He then said to me, "Ha. Whatever! You're a quitter. You know that right, that you are a quitter. That's all you do is quit things. You start then you quit just as soon as you start. So ya, go ahead. Try this whole speaking thing. You're just going to quit anyway. I can't wait to watch you quit." He was chuckling as he said it. He was smug and condescending. I sat there for a minute. I was crushed. I had no words. I had no emotion. I was just numb.

I told myself. *"See! This is why I didn't want to say anything. I didn't want to speak up. I didn't want to share!"* I knew he would be hateful, mean and crushing. Then I heard the voice again. "Get up." *"Ummm no. Did you see what just happened! I am not getting up. I'm sitting in the tub, I'm not moving and I'm not talking until he leaves."* "Get up." *"Nope. Not happening."* "Get Up! You are stronger than you think you are. Get up now!"

It wasn't a suggestion. It was a demand. I stood up. I felt strong. I grabbed a towel then wrapped it around myself and stepped out of the bathtub. I walked over to him feeling powerful and I knew he felt it as well. The look on his face said it all. He knew that something had just changed in me.

I said to him, "I am not a quitter. I have never quit anything. In the past, when I started something that you didn't like, you made me not want to continue. I would let you think I quit, by no longer talking to you about it or letting you see me. It gets too hard for me to listen to you discredit me, talk down to me, discourage me and tell me how I can't do anything. As of right now, you are wrong! The words and tone you use will no longer have power over me. You will no longer have control over me. Period! I will become a speaker! I will be great, I will be successful and I will inspire people all over the world. Watch me become a speaker! WATCH ME! WATCH ME CHOOSE ME!"

That was the day I decided I would no longer allow myself to be treated the way he was treating me. That was the day I came up with a plan to leave, so I could take my life back. Right then I decided to get out of a relationship that was about to kill me emotionally. This was where I figured out how strong I was and that God, had His hand on me. That was the day that I felt I was about to be given *"Beauty for Ashes."*

CHAPTER 5

PEACE AND WAR

Be patient. Sometimes you have to go through the worst to get to the best. - Unknown

I couldn't live in that environment anymore. I wouldn't be talked to this way anymore. I couldn't watch my youngest be miserable listening to the way he belittled me. It was changing and it was going to change now! The next night I told him I wanted to separate and he could go to his parents' empty house. We had talked about that before the trip and he said he was all right with doing that. This time around that was not the response he gave me.

He yelled "I am not going anywhere! This is my house, my stuff and I am not leaving it! If you need to fix yourself, you are the one leaving! I am not leaving this house!" Then I realized, if we were to separate, it would be me who was leaving. He told me he would call his parents and see if I could stay there. I was again doing things on his terms, not mine. His control not mine. But the difference this time, I was doing it on purpose. I needed him to think he had control of the situation. By doing so, it was going to keep me safe. The next day, he told me, "Ok, you can go. I have talked to my parents. You can leave to figure yourself out." In that conversation, he also told me what day I could leave and what I would be allowed to take. He had to have control, he couldn't release it. I was going to use that to my advantage. He needed the perception that he still had control over the situation. I didn't want him to unravel emotionally yet. I would not be able to leave on my terms if that happened.

In hindsight, his decision that I was the one leaving was a blessing in disguise. It was going to give me the extra time and opportunity to make a plan of escape. This time also allowed me to gain momentum, build up strength and manage my fears. As it got closer to the day I was leaving to go to his parents' house he was getting angrier and losing his temper constantly.

One night he completely lost it. I will never forget his emotional explosion and rage. As we were lying in bed talking, he got pissed and his face turned bright red. I thought his heart was about to burst out of his chest. His anger was just oozing out of him, even more so than normal. He stood at the foot of the bed, and yelled, "This is all your fault! You are causing this marriage to end. You are the cause of all our problems. You can't keep the girls in line, you can't keep the house picked up and you can't put the dishes away without something falling out of the cabinets. I am so tired of it! I am sick and tired of living like this! You are making my life miserable and it is all your fault. Our marriage, if it ends, it's all your fault. Every damn thing that is wrong is all your fault!"

All of his unhappiness was my fault? He was yelling at the top of his lungs. Right there for the first time, I realized this was not all my fault. It was not my fault at all. He was breathing hard, his face was beet red as he started grabbing blankets and a pillow with a huge huffing sound. He told me, "I am going to the shop to sleep, I can't look at you or be in the same bed with you. You make me sick!" He got the blankets then stormed out of the bedroom and went to the shop. That was the first time he went there to sleep. I was not sure what to think or feel. He had been so angry. He said so many things he had never said before. He actually scared me for the first time that night. I thought he would hurt himself or me. Things were definitely different this time. He felt the loss of control. His world was spinning out of control as it got closer to me leaving. Everything that he knew was unraveling. He had me so worried about his safety and mine I didn't sleep at all that night.

In the shop and all throughout the house we had guns. So I listened. I listened for doors, I listened for gunshots and I listened for anything that meant my safety was in danger. I tried to text him to check on him but of course, there was no answer. The reason I said I listened for gunshots earlier was because I thought that I might wake up to a gunshot of him shooting himself or coming into the house and shooting me. I didn't want that to happen. I was so afraid that I took out my gun and put it on the nightstand.

I knew many changes needed to happen and were about to happen. I needed some time to think for myself, to figure out my next step and to figure out what was really happening here. My eyes were so wide open now to so many things in that instant. The next night he stayed in our room. While both laid there in bed, he told me he was sorry for the things he said. I just laid there facing away from him, still afraid to go to sleep again. I was ready to get out. I kept rethinking and wondering if my plan was really going to work. I was worried if making him think he had control when he really didn't was going to backfire on me. The next night he cried and said his anxiety was through the roof. He told me

I couldn't leave him, that I needed to be there to help him. He told me he would kill himself. The anxiety was too much for him to handle. I knew if I left, he would.

I knew my plan, I knew what I was going to do. To get this done I needed to make him feel comfortable about it. To do that I had to make him think it was on his terms, when in fact it was not. It was to make it as easy as possible for him. I watched him. In the back of my mind I didn't know if he would hurt me, but I was concerned he would hurt himself. He had threatened suicide before. He started talking about it more and more. How he didn't care if our girls found him or if I found him.

He also started talking about how he should have never had me live out his fantasy. That it was clearly a mistake and breaking point for me. The fact was it was more than a breaking point, it also opened my eyes to see so much more. It showed me how he needed control of everything going on in our lives. It made me see his narcissistic type of personality. I started to figure out all of the things that he was, everything that he had been doing and what I needed to do to live my life on my terms from that point forward.

One night he was gone overnight for work. Logan was home from college and it was going to be the perfect time to talk to her. I asked myself, "Do I talk to her? Do I let her know what was happening now or wait till it gets a little closer?" I knew I was leaving and I knew when. I decided I wanted to tell Logan what was going on. She had been at college for most of the last 4 months. She had no idea what was happening at home. As she came into the bedroom, we started just talking. I thought I would drop it like a bomb because there was really nothing subtle about what I was about to say. "I am leaving your dad, I don't want to be here anymore". What she said next floored me! I couldn't have even remotely fathomed the words she would say. "Mom, you need to get the f*&k out!" she stated. "Oh my gosh! What!?" I exclaimed. She could see it. She knew what was going on. She saw all the control. She saw how he talked to me, how unhappy I was and that I was not living my best life. She saw it!

Why didn't I? Why was I so blind to it! Damn. I felt so much better just hearing her say, yes mom, go!

But wow! I had mixed feelings. I felt so much guilt. My kids witnessed this. I hadn't stopped it. I couldn't stop it because I didn't know it was happening. The guilt of letting my kids see something that was negative, but I also knew I was about to turn it all around. They would see that no matter how long you were in a relationship, it is ok to leave when it is toxic. They would know when it becomes harmful it is ok to choose you! I was going to show them that their mom was strong and was going to choose what was right for us. They would see it was a positive thing as they watched me choose me!

The day I left, I tried not to smile. I tried not to show the happy emotions I was having. I was about to be free. I was about to be released from the chains that weighed me down. I had decided to just take my clothes at that point. I would get the other things that I wanted later. He was very startled at the amount of clothes I was taking. Which is why I did just clothes. I didn't want to give him any inclination that I was leaving for good yet. Again, I didn't think he would hurt me but I wasn't 100% sure. He had been changing personalities on an hourly basis. He would go from mad, to crying, to you have to help fix me, then back to mad. He was pretty much mad all the time. I took Meghan with me. She was 11 at the time and having a very difficult time with her emotions. What she was hearing and seeing had me worried. I had no plans of ever leaving her with her dad. I wasn't sure what he was capable of doing. I didn't think he would harm her, but I still wasn't 100% sure. I didn't want to leave her there for any retaliation either. He was very mad. He would have said anything to anyone at that point. As I started packing the car, he started rambling off questions.

"How long are you going? You sure are packing a lot of clothes. You know you can come home at night and I will stay on the couch. It will be the same as you going away. You don't have to do this. I may not get through my thoughts without you here. I am going to need your help. You have to help me. When will you be back?"

He didn't know how this separation was supposed to work. We aren't supposed to communicate as much. We were taking a break from each other. He had to have a connection, the control. He was still under the assumption he had control of my thoughts and moves. He didn't, but I led him to believe that so I could leave.

He would text me all day every day. It had only been a couple of days since I had left. All his text were for me to come home, telling me he would give me space. This is why I went slowly. He would not have been able to emotionally handle being in complete control one day and zero control the next day. When I say not be able to handle it, he could feel his control slipping away. Each day he was grasping at whatever he could, his world as he knew it was falling apart.

It was a scary time for me. I was torn between my safety, his safety and Meghan's safety. I didn't cry when Meghan and I left. I felt a weight lift off of me and then I felt an inkling of relief. I came back daily to get Meghan. She would ride the bus home every day so I could pick her up before he got home. She didn't want to be around him, he was so angry at me he would yell at her and ask her questions about me. I was trying to lengthen the days between seeing him to get him accustomed to me not being there. One day I came over and did my laundry. I was trying to get it all done before he got home. That didn't happen, he came home early.

I had been gone for about 3 weeks at that point. He stood in the laundry room and told me I had to be out of his parents' house in the next few weeks. They were going to start work on their house. "You have already been gone long enough. If you stay this whole time that will give you 7 weeks to get your shit together and come back home." Get my shit together? Again, he was shifting it all on me. Trying to make me think, "It's all my fault. If I get it together, then we will be fine?" What he couldn't understand was I had no plans to ever come back there and live with him. I was out. I still needed to get the rest of my stuff, but physically I was checked out. As he said "Get my shit together" I looked at him, right in the eye, not agreeing.

He raised his voice and said, "You are not going to an apartment." I didn't say anything. I looked at him as he stated, "If you go to an apartment then our marriage is over. We will get divorced. It will most definitely be over, do you understand what I am saying?"

This conversation turned into yelling in a matter of minutes, his yelling not mine. I was calm. He yelled "You are not going to an apartment. Do you hear me!"

He felt in control as long as I was at his parent's house, where he had access to come and go as he chose. I knew that, and that was why it was working so far. I smirked at him as I turned around, got the laundry from the dryer, got Meghan and left.

The next day I put a deposit down on an apartment. I let the girls be a part of finding the apartment. We had been looking at them over the last few weeks. I had Logan come to town to look at the ones I really liked. I wanted them to like the apartment. It was going to be a place for them too. I knew it wasn't a house, I knew it wasn't going to feel like "home" to them, but I wanted them to be a part of it from the very beginning.

We found the one we all liked and picked a move in date. I needed to plan a day to go get the rest of my stuff. "What was my stuff?" I thought to myself. I didn't have anything but the rest of my clothes and pictures of the girls. Scrapbooks that I had made of them.

The day I went to gather the rest of my clothes he lost it. I had asked my friend Debra to come help me. I was afraid to be by myself and I needed help moving.

He started yelling the second we walked in the door. It was so dramatic that Debra acted like she was calling a friend to check on us. She then started recording the whole move. He yelled and hollered the whole entire time. He called me a bitch. "You are a cold-hearted fucking bitch." He yelled over and over. He said, "You never loved me. I knew you would do this to me after I opened my heart up to you in the last year." Wait, back up on that one. I said, "You have finally opened your heart up to me? We have been together for 30 freaking years and you just opened your heart up to me in the last year?" He blew my mind again. He started yelling again, you cold-hearted bitch. He followed me around, yelling in my face as I got my clothes and pictures. He kept yelling the nastiest things I had ever heard come out of his mouth. It was forty-five minutes of yelling and namecalling. Forty-five minutes of hell.

I thought it was the worst. But I was wrong. I was about to learn what a horrible person he really was. I was about to learn how vengeful and full of hate he could be. I was about to learn how he was not a good person. He was not someone who loved me. He was not someone who thought of consequences for actions.

He was not someone I could trust. He was just someone who thought of himself and him alone. His anger had now turned into something else. He hated me and he texted me every day to let me know. One night, I got over 100 texts of how much he hated me. Again, how cold-hearted I was and how he wanted to hurt me. He texted, "I hate you. I hope to hurt you as much as you have hurt me. I want to ruin your life. You are a fucking bitch." I had no idea what was about to happen. How he was out to ruin my life.

One morning, after another night of receiving hateful texts, I got a text from a friend. She told me someone she knew had found something on the internet and she was afraid to tell me. I was like, what are you talking about? "Cami. I need you to sit down. I need to know you are home and you are by yourself." she said. I am starting to freak out. "What! What do you need to tell me!" I said. I get this awful pit in my stomach. I feel like whatever she is about to say is going to be bad. "Tell me! What is it? What is going on?" She texted me a link. It was a link to a porn site. I read the link. It wasn't making sense to me. "What is this?" I asked her.

She told me to click on it. I did. I didn't even know if I had the words to explain all of the feelings that came over me at that moment. I was frozen. Was this real? What was I seeing? "OH MY GOD! That is me! OH MY GOD! Who did this? OH MY GOD!" I am screamed. I literally threw up when I saw it. I started screaming more. I started losing my shit. I was crying and screaming, and then I scrolled down. It's wasn't just one, it was about 10 videos posted of me. You could see all of me. You could see my face. You could see my whole body. You could see everything we were doing. You could see it all! I wanted to crawl up in a ball and die. Literally die, right then I wanted to die. How did this get here?? Who did this? Why did they do this! OH MY GOD! I threw up again. I seriously felt like the world had ended. I needed to just go sit in a hole and never be seen again.

I called him. I was screaming, I was yelling, I was crying and I was sick to my stomach. I said to him, "What is this? How did this get on this site! What did you do?" He was smug. He didn't care. In an evil tone. He said, "I will see what I can do. But they have been out for a long time. I put them out on websites back in

October". I said to him, "These were for you! These were not for anyone to see! Why?!? Why did you do this!!!" He just chuckled. "You made me mad. I want to hurt you. I want to ruin your life." "You did this on purpose, trying to hurt me, to destroy me, to ruin my life??" I yelled. "Yes. I want to ruin every part of your life." He told me. I was still screaming and couldn't function at that point.

Do you remember his fantasy? Remember I mentioned he had made videos, took pictures, for him only and for his pleasure he had told me. Well, when I told him I wanted to stop having sex with people he got angry. So, what did he do? He put about 20+ videos out on the world wide web. Yes, that's right, he put them all out there for the world to see. He shared them on porn sites, he swapped pictures and videos with his "internet buddies", and he gave them to more people who then uploaded them to more porn sights multiple times. Ultimately, the videos went to hundreds of thousands of people who downloaded and uploaded for six months before I even had a clue as to what he did. I had no idea they were out there.

I stayed in my apartment for the next few days. I couldn't go to work. I couldn't eat. I couldn't sleep. I couldn't get out of bed. I couldn't do anything. He did all this in an attempt to ruin me and my life. It went even further by him having conversations on these sites and in personal emails he had sent to these strangers, he had released my personal information. My full name, my website I had just started, my Facebook page information and my Twitter account. He messaged everyone or put in the comments of the videos, "Check her out and look at her new website online too." There are people to this day who know my shoe size, my clothing size and my kids' names, all kinds of private information that only he could have given out.

I finally got my composure somewhat after a few days. I had to figure out how to get these videos off the internet. This was not a simple or fast process. It would take hours to get all the emails sent out and multiple days for them to finally get taken off the porn sites. For the next few months I would find videos on a daily basis. I would also be sent messages from friends and random people I didn't know telling me about the videos. I would ask them for the links they found so I could get them removed.

I was so afraid of what would be found. Everyone was going to see these. This was going to ruin my life. I felt shame, embarrassment and fear. I walked around in fear. I shut myself down. Inside I felt like a walking zombie, I wanted to die.. I combed porn sites on a daily basis and I would find more. I would look at the comments occasionally, there were questions posted asking who I was and where they could find more videos. The number of views was astonishing, anywhere from ten thousand to three hundred thousand. I spend hours on this every day. It consumed my life.

A few months prior to discovering myself on these online sites, I had been starting my inspirational speaking quest. I was making one-minute inspirational talks on Facebook. I had also been making inspirational quotes. I had added info to my website. I was working on my dream. I started a Joyus Livin Facebook page. I posted quotes of all kinds. I was starting to make my dream real! I was laying the foundation and it was going so well. All my Facebook posts were public so everyone could see them. My friends were posting awesome feedback along with strangers. I started getting more followers. I also started getting messages that were creepy and kind of cryptic. It all made sense now. A lot of these messages were from men who had seen the videos. OH MY GOD! It was all making sense now.

I decided I needed to do something. It was getting overwhelming. There were so many each week, that I couldn't keep up. I had made friends with a couple of people who would send me pages of links on a weekly basis. I felt like it more and more were being added each day or week. I couldn't keep up. In doing more research of websites, I found another site using my name. This was different though. This was a profile of me, someone was impersonating me and I believed it was my husband. I couldn't believe it. I needed evidence to confirm it. I needed to get to his computer and make it all stop. I knew this was him, I had no evidence but I felt it. But how would I get this to stop?

I called a friend who is a police officer. I told him what was happening. He said, "We can't go get the computer unless you press charges. We would have to have a warrant." Well shit. What do I do now?" I asked

117

him. He then said, "Go get it and go get it now". He told me, "It is still your house, you are not breaking the law, you will be fine." I said ok. I was scared to go alone. "Are you home?" I asked him. "Can you sit down the street?" He told me, of all times, "I am at Frontier City with my kids!" Well of course you are! I told him I am headed that way and I have to get it. He tells me, "Be careful and text me when you go into the house and when you get out." I thought to myself, oh hell. What was I about to do? I was scared to freaking death! What if he comes home? What if he finds me in the house? He would hurt me for sure. I would be beaten to death or shot.

I drove to the house. I parked my car on a side street just down from the house behind a tree. I ran down the street and headed behind the house to the back door. My heart was racing. It was pounding through my chest. My hands were shaking. What in the hell was I doing? Oh my gosh I was about to faint. I found the key where we hid it. I opened the back door and I went inside. The dog greeted me. He was super excited to see me. Which made me forget for a second what I was doing. There were two places his computer could be. I looked in the living room beside his chair, it wasn't there. I went to the master bedroom, there it was! I found the computer! I grabbed it and the charger and headed for the back door. My heart rate had to be over 200bpm. I locked the door and put the key back where it belonged. I walked slowly to the side of the house. I look out and tried to see if anyone was coming. I walk by the garage to double check that he wasn't home. Once I saw that I was in the clear I ran for my life. I ran across the street then down to the street where I had parked my car. I got in my car and took deep breaths trying to calm myself down. My heart was pounding frantically. I literally thought I might have a heart attack in the car. My hands were still shaking. I was lightheaded and scared to death, but I was safe and I was back in my car and I had what I needed. Mission accomplished!

I knew I wouldn't be able to get in the computer. I didn't even try to open it. I knew he had it password protected since day one. I started the car and drove down the road on my way home. When I got there, I started texting him, I told him I had found a website that someone was pretending to be me. I could see they had been online just a day before. "Do you know anything about this?" I asked and he said no. He then tells me, it must be an old site or something. Hmm. I knew better and I am not buying it. I told him, "I am going to call the police. It is a felony to impersonate someone on the internet. I need to know who is behind this." I waited for a response. Nothing, he doesn't reply. I knew he was thinking. I knew he was the one doing it. I just needed him to confess. A few minutes later he confessed, "It was me." I replied, "I know and by the way, I have your computer." Silence!

I felt I was in a dilemma. I was struggling with the decision of pressing charges against him. Revenge porn is a felony in Oklahoma, he would go to prison. I didn't want my kids to grow up without their father. I also didn't want my kids to know what had happened. How do you explain that to your children? All of these thoughts were going through my mind. "What do I do?" I felt he would continue to put more videos and pictures out there. "Do I press charges? Do my kids grow up without their dad?" These were my thoughts and also my frustration. I was thinking of how it was going to affect others instead of myself!

The texting started up again. "What are you going to do with my computer. I am not going to prison. I will kill myself before I go to prison." He texted. "Wow!" I was shocked. I didn't want him to kill himself. I knew it was possibly a control tactic but I also knew he would do it if he really felt he had no other choice. I felt there was no way the porn would stop being added to the internet unless I pressed charges. I wanted it to stop. I was so tired of trying to get it taken down daily. There had to be a way to make it stop. I texted him and told him to meet me at Panera Bread. It was a place where there would be plenty of witnesses. I would be safe and he wouldn't do anything in public. But just in case, I called for backup, I had a friend of mine meet me there. I wanted them to sit at another table and make sure everything was fine.

I got his text, "I'm here, you don't have police inside do you? If you do, I will shoot myself in the truck right now." I texted back to him, "No, I don't have the police here. I just want you to come inside, log on to your computer and delete everything. I want you to sign an affidavit that you will not post anything else from this point on. If you do, I will file charges and you will go to prison." He finally came inside and we sat at a booth. This was the first time I had seen him in months. The sound of his voice, his body language, his movement and his overall demeanor was now an instant emotional and physical trigger that made my skin crawl. Seeing him or being around him made me nauseous and want to throw up. I needed this meeting to go quickly and be over so all these feelings would go away.

I handed him his laptop and the external drives that I had found. "Open it" I said. My voice was angry and had a forceful tone. As he opened it, he logged in and went to all the files. He deleted everything on his laptop, everything on the drives. I watched him delete it all, including the trash bin folders. He started talking as he was erasing the files on his laptop. He told me, "This is so sad, all this great footage is being destroyed. All these moments will be gone forever. This is such a waste. It makes me sick that it is all gone forever." Tears started rolling down my cheeks. His voice was angry and all the feelings of anxiousness and panic I had felt in our marriage were slowly creeping back inside me. My friend at the table across the room started to get up. I motioned for him to sit. I was ok. All of these emotions I had pushed down for the last few months surfaced in minutes. Bam! Every word he spoke took me back to a period I wanted to erase, just as all the videos and pictures were being erased from his laptop. I wanted it erased from my memory, my hard drive in my head. The reality was it would never be erased in my head.

Having all the files deleted made me feel better. I couldn't think past what was happening at that moment and how I got him to erase it all. How it made me feel, it felt good at that moment. I had control of the situation. I took some of my power back. It felt good. I was so proud of myself. I did something for me, for myself. It was all finished now. He looked at me with hate and said, "It's done. I fucking hate you." He took his computer and left. I sat there for a moment and then the flood of emotions came crashing in. I let the tears flow. My friend came over to my table. I told him, "Thank you, I appreciate you coming to make sure I was safe." I got in my car and drove home.

The reality was I didn't get much accomplished that day. I thought I had, but the more I thought about it the more I really realized I didn't. I just made it harder for him to get to it. All he had to do was go back to the emails he sent and save them. All he had to do was message all the people he messaged and get them back. They were probably already on his profiles on all his porn sites. I didn't accomplish much of anything. At the time those thoughts never entered my mind. I was just in the moment of getting them deleted off his laptop. I didn't see the big picture.

His goal was to ruin me. My goal was to make it all go away without killing me emotionally. He was not succeeding, but what he was doing was making my life a living hell. The outside world didn't see what was brewing inside me, what was causing me pain. I wanted to press charges but felt I could not without it affecting my kids. I wasn't thinking clearly, I wasn't thinking about me. All I could think of was my children without their Dad, not the terrible things their dad had done to their Mom. Ultimately the biggest factor in my decision to not pressing charges was that I did not want my kids to find out about the videos and what their dad have me do. I had no doubt, he would have manipulated the story to his benefit. How would I explain any of this to them? I felt so much shame and embarrassment. They would judge me or they would hate me. This was where my head was constantly. I couldn't press charges for these reasons. I couldn't face my kids, I was ashamed and feared their judgment.

I was so afraid of my friends, family and colleagues finding out, I shut down my Facebook pages. My Cami Martin page, my Joyus Livin Facebook page, my Instagram and Twitter. I turned them all off. I stopped doing my online inspirational videos too. Random men were still messaging me saying they had seen my videos, telling me they wanted to see more and making sexually explicit comments. I was blocked people daily. I lived in so much fear.

CHAPTER 6

OVERCOMING

Forgive yourself for not knowing better at the time. Forgive yourself for giving away your power. Forgive yourself for the survival patterns and traits you picked up while enduring trauma. Forgive yourself for being who you needed to be.

—AUDREY KITCHING

How do I move forward from here? How do I live my life? I knew I needed to think differently, I had shut down. I needed to look inward and to look past so much hurt in myself to see the good things. There were good things! I was freed from this marriage and that was a great thing. Looking back, it was like I was freed from a prison which I didn't even know I was in at the time. This was also a great thing. I had made so many new friends and had many other friends that were supporting me through my divorce.

My friends reminded me I was a great person, I was beautiful, I was fun to be with and that I inspired when I listening to them. They told me I was a great friend. I started seeing myself differently. I was changing my mindset. I was a beautiful person! I was a strong person and I was fun to be around! I had so many friends from social and work life that saw the real me. The way that I should have been seeing myself.

The words I had been told for years about myself were not true. His words used to tear me down while lifting himself up. During this time I also learned I had fight in me and I knew how to fight back. Before my reactions to conflict or hurtful situations was to flee or freeze. I figured out I had been using a flight response most of my life. I needed to flee for my safety and protection. Realizing this was huge in my healing. I figured out additionally why I had so much shame for myself. I felt shame for all videos that were still out there and being seen. It was never meant for anyone to see except him. The pain in my heart I was having to face, all the emotions and all the feelings were there so I could heal.

I figured it out one day. It came down to one word that was crippling me and it was causing me not to move forward. I came to the realization that it wasn't shame; it was fear. Fear, an ugly word that is crippling and debilitating. In that reflection it was fear that I felt. A huge fear that I would fight every time I found a video, or if someone sent me information on a video. Fear had its hold on me so tight over the past few years. Fear of someone finding out, someone seeing it or someone judging me for it. Fear is horrible! It takes away your power. Fear is also not the truth, it holds you back from what is real. It holds you back from reality and the truth. You have to face your fear, know your truth. By knowing your truth, by facing your fear you get your power back.

So, what was I fearful of? I was fearful of people finding out. How do I face that fear to take my power and control back? I tell my story. I tell people what happened, even the ugly stuff. By doing this, neither him, the fear nor anyone else has power over me. I hold all the power.

The first thing I did to take that power back, I told my girls. That was a big one, it was a hard one too. I told them everything. Logan was 21 and dating. People of all ages watch porn, what if one of her friends said: "Hey, I saw your mom." I can't imagine how she would have responded to that comment. What would that conversation have looked like with her having to confront me? I had been struggling over the last 4 years living in fear of them finding out about the videos. I was worried sick that someone would say something to them. I had to tell them so I would be free of that fear and prepare them for the consequences of their dad's actions.

I wasn't sure how they would respond. What would they say, what would they think? Would they judge, would they think I was weak? Talking myself into telling them was such a struggle. It was something I thought about constantly for years. Would they understand? I knew I had to tell them. I knew it was finally time. The book was almost done, there were more videos being posted continuously. It was time.

I asked Logan to meet me for breakfast. I wanted to throw up. I was shaking and I told her I was about to tell her something she couldn't un-hear. I was sorry I was having to have this whole conversation. She had no idea what I was about to say and I was scaring her. I told her as my marriage deteriorated, I wanted to fix things, like I always do. I just matter of fact said, "Your dad wanted me to have sex with other men to fix our marriage, so I did." She listened as I explained to her how it started. I informed her it went on for a while but then it got bad. Then I said, I am having to tell you this because your dad got so mad when I wanted to stop doing it that he put a lot of videos out on the internet. I have tried my best to get them taken down, but they will never be gone. In fact, I am all over the internet at any given time. I email the sites and get them taken down when I find out about them, but I don't always know when they get put up. It may be days, weeks or months before I find them.

Logan was surprised but handled it amazingly well. I made it clear to her that there was a possibility that one of her friends might see them and say something to her. I needed her to be prepared if it happened. Let me just say now, that my daughter is awesome. Our conversation covered why I didn't press charges against her dad. I let her know that I wanted him to be part of their life. Her response shocked me, "I would have pressed charges mom." I also told her that he threatened to kill himself. That didn't surprise her either. "If he did mom, that is his choice. It would not be on you."

It was a great conversation that initially I was so afraid to have with her. I had been living in fear that she would think a certain way. It was not the truth. She didn't judge me at all. She was glad I told her. As I was informing her of everything, I was envisioning giant silver chains wrapped around my arms, binding my arms to my sides, holding me captive. The more I shared with her the more I envisioned them breaking away and sliding down my arms. I felt the weight of the fear finally release me. It was the best feeling. I felt my power as it rose up inside me, I was empowered.

Next, I told Meghan, that was another shocking conversation for me. My Meg is a giant hearted person. She feels so much for everyone. She has so much empathy. I wasn't sure how to approach her. I decided to tell her while we were en route to a birthday party. It wasn't the best timing but a segue had emerged and I needed to take it. I told her the same thing I said to Logan. I explained why I didn't press charges; I wanted your dad in your life and tears started rolling down her face. It was hurting my heart. She was ok though. She wasn't sad and she understood. The next thing she said though I was not prepared for. She advised me that a lot of kids watch porn. She didn't watch but it was very prevalent in kids her age. I couldn't believe her statement, then she said she needed to say something, but she didn't know how. I said to write it down. I had mentioned the term Hot Wife to her when I was telling her about it all. It was a lifestyle some people were involved in and I did not define it. She then wrote on a piece of paper. "My dad is a cuck?" I nearly died then I asked her, "How do you even know that term?" I told her no he wasn't. He wanted to be but his need for power and control was too strong. Plus I couldn't talk to him or anyone that way.

Those were conversations I will never forget, either one of them. I went in with the fear of not knowing what they would think or say. I feared the shame and judgment, but they didn't judge or shame me. They completely understood. They understood way more than I ever imagined they could. They even gave me advice on what they would have done in that situation. It was a conversation I dreaded and put off a lot longer then I should have. In doing so, I let all kinds of thoughts and anxieties build up in my head. These were all based on fear. None of which were real! After I faced the biggest fear of telling them, I felt I could share my story with anyone now. I got back my power by facing my fears and telling the truth. I felt these words come over me.

I am beautiful!

I am powerful!

I am strong!

I could feel those words wanting to roar out of me. I am walking in truth with no fear. I am walking in truth with my head high to help others face their own fear and grow.

Know your truth!

Face your fear!

Feel your power!

CHAPTER 7

POWER & CONTROL
THE WHEEL OF
ABUSE

When a flower doesn't bloom you fix the environment it grows in, not the flower -

Unknown

During my marriage, before I was fully aware of my situation, I started coming to the realization of what truly happened to me. I asked a friend of mine to join me for lunch. I mentioned to her that I was trying to figure out the "how" in my plan for leaving. We talked about most of the things that had occurred, but I didn't share with her or anyone about the sexual abuse back then. After I explained my story, she told me her story. I had never heard it. I was floored! I couldn't believe what she had been through. I had known her for years but never knew much about her life. While visiting with her an unfamiliar word surfaced, Narcissist. I googled it. I read the definition multiple times. Wow, this was the type of personality trait I had married! Then I looked up domestic violence. I broke down in tears. I was living a marriage of domestic violence in multiple forms. As I read, I found out all the different forms of abuse. I didn't even know most of them existed. I was a victim and he was a perpetrator. At that point, I started doing a lot of research.

I figured out a plan to leave based on what his reactions would be to my actions. This research came into play often, as it helped me determine how he might react to things I said or would do. I kept saying these words to myself again and again, "I was the victim. He was a perpetrator." You might be asking yourself, "What was I a victim of?" I was a victim of mental, emotional, financial and sexual abuse. I was a victim of a violent controlling domestic relationship. I did not do anything to cause this situation. I would not own any shame in being a victim. I was not the cause of this martial downfall and abuse. I would not allow those feelings to have power over me and I would tell my story. I would tell it from the mindset of being a survivor of domestic violence. I am a survivor of the sexual, financial, mental and emotional abuse. I had to learn what all that meant and also the emotions and triggers that existed within me.

I went through training at the YWCA on domestic violence. It made me see so clearly what type of marriage I had been in. It helped me understand more about the different types of abuse of which I was a victim. You are probably aware of most types of abuse discussed there. The one that was new and eye opening to me was the financial abuse. I didn't even know there was such a thing. It is a real thing to see, the perpetrator generally spends money on themselves and the victim is never allowed to spend money on anything. This was what happened to me all the time. You may remember that he told me, what we lacked financially was my fault because I never made enough money. I wasn't allowed to buy anything, he could of course, buy motorcycles, guns, 4-wheelers, hunting equipment, tools, and all kinds of other machinery. Wow, this was a huge thing! I felt validated now knowing this information.

An example of how I wasn't allowed to spend money. I had a car wreck in 2011 where I received a substantial settlement. He wanted two things, a motorcycle and for me to have a breast augmentation. In all fairness, I wanted the augmentation also. But what I didn't want was the breast size he desired. As far as he was concerned, I could have the breast size that he wanted or none at all so I went with his size. So the day the money was deposited, he took my settlement money and used it to pay for his motorcycle.

Later when it was time for my surgery, I had to put it on my credit card which I had to work to pay off later. He would again tell me it was because "We didn't have enough money."

I wasn't allowed to buy anything for myself, period. The reason why I only took my clothes and pictures was that I didn't have anything else to take. I had nothing there that was mine. I owned nothing but my car. I even tried to take kitchen utensils and he told me to put them back, he bought those. My clothes were the only thing that were truly mine.

These are all pieces of financial abuse. I was told that all of our financial struggles were my fault, but it wasn't true. Once I had moved out and was living on my own, I had money left over. My bills were higher now. My expenses were higher. Why did I have money all of a sudden? How was that possible? How had he really spent our money? I struggled for a long time with money being a negative trigger for me. I didn't want to see what was in my checking account. I didn't like the feeling I associated with money and bills. It took a long time to rewire my brain to understand that I was going to have enough. I could pay my bills. I could look at my checking account without having a huge panic attack or feel all of those negative feelings associated with that fear. I was going to have more than enough. You are doing fine, better than fine. It was so crazy looking back at how paying bills or looking at my checking account balance made me feel a certain way. It always gave me anxiety. I wasn't going to have enough money or I didn't know how to manage money, he would tell me. All of those nasty things he used to say I rung out in my head every time I paid my bills. It was debilitating. I never knew why until then. It was another trigger. A trigger that reminded me of those past negative experiences, like a flashback, that would bring up all the feelings of fear and panic that would cause me to be anxious, nervous and avoid that event. I could work through it and I would work through it.

The emotional and verbal abuse had been daily. His tone of voice, the words he spoke to me. Remember the riding lawnmower story? That was emotional and verbal abuse. He didn't want me to be happy doing my thing, living my life basically. Therefore, he would make me feel bad by verbally attacking me so he could feel better. He revealed his need for power and control at its finest.

If something was wrong, broke, or wasn't going the right way, he would yell out cuss words before he hit whatever might be broken or was close to him. These outbursts caused me to freeze or caused me to flee. It caused me to walk on eggshells and stressed me out. As time went on, he started getting mad every day and no matter what the real reason for his anger was, he would always say it was my fault.

The girls and I would stop for snacks and drinks when we would go places in the car like to practice, games, or wherever. We did this regularly especially if it was a long trip. I believe most people would think this was normal. When all four of us would get into a car to travel I knew he wouldn't stop so I packed a snack bag. It would make him so mad. "You have trained them to think they have to eat or drink something every time we get into the car." In his warped mind, I had made them into monsters because they had to constantly eat and drink in the car. "No, I have made it to where they have a snack, a drink and entertainment as we drive for 12 -14 hours" I would say. "This is your fault that they act like this and need these things," he would yell back.

One year, we were in Denver, Colorado while Logan was playing in a softball tournament. We played in this tournament every year. We were going back and forth for meetings, games and practice to the team hotel. We didn't stay at the team hotel at this tournament. We stayed in our travel trailer outside of town. It was less expensive. All the other tournaments we played it would be Logan and I that traveled. At those times, we would stay at the same hotel as the team so that we could share a hotel room with other players and parents. We enjoyed hanging out with the players and their families on other trips. But Colorado was different because it was very expensive and a weeklong tournament. We turned each trip there into a family vacation.

One night the players and parents were going to meet. Logan and I wanted to stop off and see everyone at the hotel for a bit before we went back to the campsite. She and I were very social people and he was not. He, of course, would make us feel bad and wrong for wanting to socialize versus going back to camp. He started arguing with me about why I always had to have people around. He would constantly say, "Why can't you just do nothing? Logan and you always have to keep the road hot and go to places to see people. Why do you have to act like that?" He made us feel abnormal because we enjoyed being around other people. We were wrong or doing something wrong just because we wanted to be around people. As we were driving and discussing why we would like to stop, he got so mad because it wasn't what he wanted to do. He lost it. He lost his temper in the truck as we were driving. He took his fist and hit the dash of the truck. He continually slammed his fist into the dash while yelling at the same time. I jumped. I had tears well up in my eyes. The girls started crying. Then he yelled at us and told us he was never coming back again. He said we were acting like we didn't want him around and we didn't want him to be there. That wasn't it at all. All we wanted was to go see the team, the families. It wasn't like we were asking to stay in the hotel with the team, we just wanted to join them for dinner. It was the exact opposite of what he liked, so that made us bad people for wanting to be social.

We were constantly ridiculed for wanting to go places and do things. "You have to keep the road hot don't you, you can't just stay home and do nothing." As I look back now, I see, all he wanted to do was sit in a recliner and watch tv, be served food, or cook and eat by himself than go to bed. It was my fault according to him that Logan liked to "keep the road hot" like me. It was my fault that we had fun outgoing kids.

I realized it was after the girls were born, that was time when the verbal abuse really started happening more and more. If he got mad at something then it was taken out on me. Somehow, someway it was my fault, or he would come inside to yell at me about something else that wasn't to his liking then go back outside. If he was mad or miserable, then the whole crew would need to be miserable. He would come in and yell at everyone, for things that were so small they didn't even matter. The trash cans! This was the girl's responsibility. To bring them to the side of the house on trash day. They would forget. He literally would come inside yelling at the top of his lungs at how sick and tired he was at repeating himself on the trash cans then he would hit something like the couch, the chair or he would kick whatever was near him. The girls would cower down, I would freeze. He would walk out the door and I would talk to them to make it better. Yes, they needed to get the trash cans, but they didn't need to feel they were worthless for forgetting. His goal was to make us all upset so he could feel better. He would be happy. I would whisper to the girls many times over the years after the things he did to tell them, "It's ok, don't worry." I remember telling them "I'm sorry he is acting this way" because they didn't understand why. They would ask, "Why does he say these things to you mom?" And I would reply, "I don't know, he is just upset about work, or upset about something." In hindsight I spent many years of my life making excuses for him.

He said many things to me and them. His other favorite phrase I have mentioned was, "So you finally decided to come home!" This statement would make me so mad while hurting me deeply at the same time. It would not matter if I had taken one of the girls to a friend's house or to practice, it was what he said every time I came home. I hated it. Sometimes I would go to the gym and not come home till 7 pm. I didn't want to be there and hear all the hateful words he would say.

The pain we go through as victims doesn't have to be physical to leave marks. It doesn't have to be physical to leave scars. I have scars, emotions and feelings that trigger my pain. These triggers can be anything that I see, hear and experience that remind me of past events that caused that pain. Those triggers would bring back that pain and cause me to freeze up again. It may be a word that someone says, it may be a text tone that someone may have that I hear playing. I have scars that will take a while to heal. I sometimes find triggers that I never even realized that I had. Over the last few years, things trigger me less and less. As the years go by, I am hopeful that I will continue to break free of them. Some will never totally go away. Instead of reacting to them, I have learned to respond to them. They pop up in the most unlikely places.

CHAPTER 8

EMERGING

Rise Up and become the person YOU were

meant to be. - Dieter F. Uctdorf

Let's talk about what happened to me after I left. Let's talk about the changes that have taken place. Let's talk about how I got to where I am today as I write this book. Let's talk about me emerging! It has been an incredible journey.

After I left, when I had been gone for about two weeks, I remember this one particular moment where I woke up in the middle of the night. I had a thought come into my head. You could call it an epiphany, you could call it God talking to me, you could call it all sorts of things. I would definitely call it a freeing statement, a healing statement.

My daily routine no longer consists of worrying about, will this make him happy or mad.

Boom! That isn't a big statement to most, but it was a huge statement for me. I literally sat up, turned on the light, rolled over and grabbed my phone. I went to my note pad app and typed it in. I wanted to remember exactly what was said in my head. I wanted to also remember the feeling of when I repeated it to myself, how it felt. How I felt! Wow, the rush of the feelings, relief, calmness and freedom. Peace!

Softball had just started and the season took my mind off a lot of things and made my daily life easier. Logan was a freshman at college. One of the first tournaments was in Palm Springs, so I decided I would go! I should definitely go and getaway. Great weather, a place I had never been to before. It would be great! Perfect for my mind and perfect to watch my kid play. On the first game day, I had a few hours to kill before the games started. I decided to go to a coffee shop that I had found while out exploring. It had a large courtyard where the sun shined directly on to the beautiful soft green grass. There were Adirondack chairs and benches all around it where you could sit and enjoy your day. People were walking their dogs, sitting on some of the benches. It was a beautiful morning. The sun was shining, the air was crisp and I had a notebook and a pen. I remember texting my dad and telling him where I was, how beautiful it was and how at peace I was feeling.

I wanted to write. I wanted to make a list. I wanted to list all the things I liked to do. All the things

149

I wanted to do! I love lists! Yes! I got my coffee and found the perfect chair in the sun. I pulled out my pen and pad, I was ready! A few minutes later I was looking at a blank piece of paper. Well hmmm, Um, why can't I write? I had come to an impasse. I had come to this conclusion in just a few minutes and it was really hard to accept. I couldn't write the things I liked or wanted to do. Why? I didn't know what they were. Read that again. I didn't know what they were. I didn't know what I liked. I didn't know what I wanted to do.

The realization was I was not allowed to make my own decisions in so long that I had no idea what I liked or didn't like. If you don't make those decisions for yourself, you don't know what the damn answers are. This is really sad. I thought about the things I had done over the last 30 years. Did I enjoy these things I used to do? Was I just going because I was excited to go somewhere? Hmmm. I liked going to Colorado on vacation because it was beautiful. My first choice would definitely have been the beach though! Oh, I just gave myself an answer. I liked the beach. You got one! You like and want to go to the beach! Yes! In my 30 years of being married, he and I only went to the beach once because it was a free trip. He never left the cabana and he read magazines the whole time. That was not what I wanted to do on the beach.

Ok, what's next. I proceeded to make a list of places or foods I liked. Types of movies or movies I wanted to see. Places I had wanted to go see. I was smiling! It was good. It felt good. By the time I had finished I had a good list of things I liked and wanted to do. Keyword, things "I" liked and wanted to do. Me! Things I wanted. No one else. I could go by myself or with someone, but this was a list of what I wanted to do. Yeah! This was a big progress for me. Small but it was me moving forward. The trip was only for 2 days. It was just enough to start thinking, watch some softball, relax and have some quality alone time at a beautiful place.

I went back home and continued to make lists. I continued to think about things that inspired me. What do I love...? I had a lot of alone time now to rediscover myself. I needed to figure out how to love myself again. I was actually doing better than I thought I was. I was doing a lot of reflecting. What was I happy with?

What did I need to do better? How did I feel when I looked at myself in the mirror?

When I made the decision to leave my husband I grew. I am not sure I can describe what that means. I actually grew before I left. I started gaining so much strength and momentum it was difficult to recognize my own self sometimes. The changes I saw were that good. I can remember one day very clearly. I was standing in the garage with my husband. I don't remember why I was there. I was very calm, very much in control of myself and all my emotions. We were having a conversation, It was about me coming back. How he couldn't do life by himself. How he couldn't think about not kissing me ever again. How he would never hold me again. How only I could fix him. I couldn't leave and not give him a chance to fix himself. I was dressed in heels and a nice outfit, I had been at work. I walked over to him. I was in his space. I proceed to say, "No. I am not coming back. No! I cannot fix you. You have to fix yourself and get yourself together for yourself. No one else. I will not be coming back, ever! This is not where I live anymore. Shortly I will no longer be married to you and we will be moving forward. I cannot help you." I didn't have tears, I wasn't sad, I wasn't mad. I was matter of fact. It was a new feeling. I was so proud of myself. I could stand up for myself, I was strong, I was stronger and more powerful than I even knew. I stood up for me.

I was healing while I was finding my strength. I was continuing to find joy and happiness. I was growing daily. In my growth came more strength, more joy, more peace along with gratefulness, happiness and most of all love. Love of myself. I loved myself. Who I was and who I was becoming. It was a beautiful thing.

CHAPTER 9

FINDING

LOVE

I fell in love with him not because he silenced all of my fears or made me feel so safe: I fell in love with him because he awoke a sleeping lioness within me – A wild woman who knows only passion and freedom and laughs away her fears. - Unknown

In the midst of loving myself, being transparent and genuine, love found me. It was not what I was expecting or looking for. In fact, the feelings freaked me out. I had met a man who was a friend at first. I was not looking for a relationship and neither was he. I met him on the dance floor one night while out with friends. His name was Charles. We began talking every now and then, chatting about everything. We didn't see each other or talk every day because we lived in different cities. He actually lived about an hour or so away and when I found out what he did as a career I was like, oh no. We can't talk anymore. He laughed and asked me why. I told him because you work where my daughter goes to school. You may know my daughter! This was too close for comfort. I didn't want my daughter to run into us if I went on a date with him. Which was stupid, but I wasn't ready for her to know I was beginning to date. Most people didn't even know I was getting divorced or left my husband at this point. I stopped talking to him for a bit. He understood, gave me my space but didn't give up. We wanted to meet for drinks and dancing so we eventually agreed. It was an amazing night. It went so well that we met for coffee the next morning before he left town. We sat at a Starbucks nearby and just talked. It was easy, smooth and natural. It was unbelievable! There was something so amazing about this man. I wanted to find out more about him but at the same time I was also hesitant.

I was getting divorced. I didn't need to be catching feelings! Run! I told myself, **but I didn't.**

We talked a lot. I didn't see him but maybe once every few weeks, but we talked all the time. There was something so intriguing about him. So open that we could talk for hours. It would be both of us taking turns talking and listening. It was an incredible experience, a new experience for me. I was a completely different person with him. I was letting him meet the real me. The vulnerable me that I hadn't let anyone meet. Even my girls were slowing getting used to the new me. It was a change for them as well. "Mom was picking herself over anyone else, including US!" I am sure that is what they were both thinking. That was definitely different for them. I was telling them no more often to things that I normally would have said yes. I was also answering their requests with no more when it came to things I needed to do for myself. I was finally choosing me.

Charles, just typing his name right now makes me smile. His name makes me smile like a lovesick teenager. He was a blessing that walked into my life and I had no idea what was about to transpire. When we were together, even at the very beginning, time stood still. We had a connection that was insane from the start. I don't know how to explain it. I tried to not fall for him. I tried so hard. I cried a few times because I wasn't sure what was happening to my heart. "Feelings? Oh no! I can't have these. Oh Lord, Jesus in heaven make these feelings go away. I don't want feelings! I am not ready to have feelings"

My next thoughts were, he probably doesn't feel the same. We had both agreed initially that we were not looking for a relationship. I couldn't help the negative thoughts from coming. "He doesn't have feelings for me. This is one sided. What do I do?" I kept thinking this is bad, very bad.

He would come to town with friends and we would all meet. I remember one instance very clearly.

It was his birthday weekend and he invited me to his birthday party. I was so excited to celebrate with him and his friends. The next day was his actual birthday and I had already bought him a card and a strawberry cupcake. I remembered in one of our many conversations that he liked strawberry cake. Of course, he did, so did I.

I didn't stay at his party very long. I needed to go home; Meghan was home. I wanted to stay but I also felt very uncomfortable there. Leaving was best so I drove home and realized I was upset. Very upset! I really didn't understand all the emotions I was having then. I didn't like feeling so vulnerable, so open, but at the same time, I knew it was something I needed to feel so I could grow as a person. I needed to be able to feel. He and I hadn't been talking for very long but, ugh! How could I already feel so much for him? How could this be happening. I remember that drive home where I asked God to take it away. I wasn't looking for a relationship. I didn't think it was the best timing. But God had other plans. He didn't take any of it away. God just made it stronger. We met up the next day so I could give him his card and cupcake. It made me smile so big seeing him. He told me thank you, he didn't have a cake and that it meant a lot to him. Seeing him made my heart happy.

I had started noticing when we were together things were so different from anything that I had ever experienced. I noticed new things with him every time we were together. Eating for example, let's just say, I will never eat pizza and chicken wings again without thinking of how we ate them together for the first time in front of Little Caesars. It was magical! We were magical together. I started seeing little things too. When we would see each other, we would kiss, but it was different, our breathing would sync. I started noticing it wasn't just our breath, it was our heartbeats. It was our stride when we walked or ran. Oh, and our thoughts, we could answer each other's questions and finish each other's thoughts. It was freaky but incredible.

Our relationship continued to fall into place as time went on. We didn't set out to date each other, it wasn't in our plans to have a relationship. It just flowed. We started seeing each other more and more often. He would come to the city to see me. I would go to his house to see him. It just happened. We shared everything.

When we would go out, he would ask me where do you want to go? "Um, ugh! I don't know" is what I would say. He wanted me to choose where we would go. He wanted my input. I would have no idea. It was still hard for me to make decisions. What if he didn't like the place I chose? One night, we sat on the couch and he said, "You need to decide where we are going." "I'm sorry I need to do what?" I said. I was almost laughing as I said it. It was a crazy statement. I can't make those decisions. I actually didn't know at the time that I wasn't capable of making those decisions. It literally gave me anxiety. He said to me, "You decide where we are going. I can give you a list of places if you need them, but you get to pick. You need to be able to decide what you want. We aren't leaving until you decide where we are going." Who was he I thought to myself. Do people like you really exist? How is it that this man came into my life at this time to help me grow in areas where I didn't know I needed growth.

Every time we went somewhere in the beginning I had to decide. He didn't want me to just say ok that sounds good to whatever he had suggested. He knew my history. We had talked a lot about my past. He was so understanding, he never judged nor made me feel less of a person.

It was so hard for me to make those choices for the longest time. It slowly got easier. I got to the point where I could say, hey babe, I would like to go do this. I no longer needed suggestions! It felt so good to know what I wanted! Today, he still will say, I need to know what you want. I can decide and I am able to tell him without fear and anxiety. Sometimes it is hard to not revert back to the old ways. I am a pleaser and a giver. Still to this day, I want to make sure he likes where we are going or what we are doing. The difference is now I know how to say no to something. In the past that was never an option.

My favorite thing to do with him is dance. We found a couple of places to go and became regulars. Making lots of new friends along the way. We found out we had a love for Latin music and Latin dances. I thought we had something crazy when we would sync up from being apart, until we danced. Oh my! We would have strangers come up to us regularly complimenting us how great we are together. They would say how they felt our love and our passion for each other as we danced. It still makes me smile when we hear these comments.

Our love has grown. My hope is that you get to know and experience this type of love in your lifetime. The type of love that gives you butterflies in your stomach and takes your breath away. Neither one of us were looking for a relationship, much less to fall in love. It just grew into the absolute best thing I have ever felt in my life. This man is all about the little things. He wants to make sure he does things that make me happy. That make me smile. Oh, how he makes me smile. One day, I got to thinking to myself, he does so many things out of the ordinary. It made me wonder, how much more does he do in comparison to most men? I started writing things down as he did them. It turned into a long list. I called it "An amazing man..." I sent it to him one day after we had been dating for about a year. He couldn't believe it. I told him, "Baby, these are all the little things about you that I am so grateful for and the list is bigger than this, but I am running out of paper." Here is a small example of what I sent him.

An amazing man…

> Holds my hand when I am sleeping…
>
> Kisses my hand as he holds it…
>
> Slows my breathing, my heart rate, settles me…
>
> Tells me his thoughts, hopes and dreams…
>
> Picks me up with words that are 100% on point…
>
> Wants to make a difference in people's lives…
>
> Protects me…
>
> Can stop me in my tracks with a smile that lights up the room.
>
> Sends me songs during the day that makes my heart skip a beat.
>
> Makes me personalized cards that require scissors and glue!

CHAPTER 10

MY KING, MY EXTRA AND RACISM

You will know your king, not by how he dresses or what he spends on you. No, you'll know your king by how he leads you, and loves you. - unknown

I mentioned early in this book that God gave me extra when I was born. God knew I was going to go through some stuff, some major trauma! He has given me extra positivity to look at the world differently than most. He has given me extra height so I can see the people from a different view. He has given me extra love in Charles so I can see love in a way that I never knew was possible nor that I ever believed I was capable of giving or receiving.

Through this journey of finding myself, I found a love that is indescribable. It touches all of my 5 senses. It is a love that helps you grow as a person. It is a love that isn't jealous of others, or each other's past. A love that allows us to share our past and present stories with each other to learn who we are and how we got there. It is real, it is deep and it is powerful. It is a love that is like nothing I could have even come close to imagining. It is better than anything I would have ever been able to dream. It is true!

I believe that Charles is my extra. He adds to me and to my life. He does not fill something that I was missing in my heart, that I did for myself. That is what makes him my extra. He adds to my heart and we complement each other. He has helped me grow, helped me face fears and helped me understand myself. He is compassionate, he is loving, he is caring, he is genuine and he is passionate. He has helped me see the world through his eyes and his perspective. He has helped me understand relationships. How we can be fantastic by ourselves and how we can be super fantastic as a team. Many of our friends refer to us as "The Power Couple."

As I grew in myself, I was able to see the truth in another person in my life differently. A man I held dear to my heart and I loved so very much, my Dad. It was accidental, unplanned and much to my disappointment what I found out about him.

When I called my dad and told him I was leaving my ex-husband, his exact words were "Well it's about damn time!" I was in shock with those words when they came out of this mouth. He was so happy I had finally seen my ex for the person he really was and hated what I had been put through. He had always been there to support me from as early as I can ever remember. He was a rock that was steady in my life. I knew he loved me greatly, he told me every day. We were so close that we talked and texted daily. He was my Dad and I just knew he was the best. I loved him immensely.

The last weekend in September I had mentioned to my dad and my stepmother that I was seeing someone. I told them he was awesome. At the end of the text to my stepmother I shared a picture of us. "Oh, he is handsome," she said. "Yes, he is!" I responded. Nothing else was said except talk to you later and we moved on. On October 2nd things were about to change and I had no idea what was about to happen. It was a Monday and I was headed to Shawnee where I was working that day. I called my Dad on the drive there. He says, "Hello, I have been waiting for you to call." It was a voice I almost didn't recognize. Was he mad, sick, hurt? His voice sounds really weird. Hmm Ok. "What's going on?" I asked. "You don't know?" he replied. I proceeded to tell him, "I have no idea." He then started a conversation that I will remember for the rest of my life. "I need to know what is going on. What on earth are you doing? Do you not value your job or your life?" he says. At this point I am completely confused and have no clue what he is talking about.

"Your boyfriend" he said. "Yes, Charles, what about him?" With a raised voice he exclaimed, "You are dating a black man!" What he said next resembled this, "What are you thinking? I will tell you what you are not thinking! You are not thinking about your life! You are going to ruin your life! You are going to run your life into the ditch! You are going to lose your job and you are going to lose your kids and then have no life! Your life is literally going to be in the ditch!!" He is now yelling at me. I am silent. I have tears running down my face. I have no words. I am dumbfounded. What is he saying and why is he saying it?

At this point I am in total shock. I continued to be silent. I catch my breath then I try to find the words that were bouncing around in my head, as I respond with, "What in the world are you talking about? Nothing that you just said is reality. Charles is an amazing man and you haven't even met him!" He then said, "I don't want to meet him. I don't want to have lunch with him. I don't want to get to know him!" Wow! What is truly happening in this conversation? "This relationship is a choice. And if you choose to continue to be in it then I will no longer be there for you. I will no longer support you in any way including financially if you need it." As he tells me this, I think to myself, did he just give me an ultimatum? Did he really just tell me that I could choose him or Charles? Is this for real? I sat there in silence for a moment. I expressed to him "I'm sorry, but I can't talk to you anymore at this point. I have to go" then I hung up.

As I continued my drive to work, I can't stop crying. I can't believe this conversation. I got through the day in a fog. I went home and I continued turning the conversation over and over in my mind. Trying to wrap my mind around all the things that he said. I couldn't sleep that whole night. I have all these things I want to say to him. I know I would not be able to tell him over the phone because my emotions were on overdrive and the tears would get in the way. I would not have been able to get it all out. I had to get it all out. I had to say everything that was on my mind. So, I decided to send him a long text message from my phone. It was long but it said everything I felt. I wanted to see what his response was going to be to my message. Here is what I texted him:

I've been going over our conversation most of the day and all night. I slept not one minute I'm still actually in shock with most of it. Getting past the shock, it has me thinking. Lots of thoughts but the most prevalent ones are you're not happy with my choice, you're not having any part of it and you're embarrassed and appalled about the whole situation.

I'm the happiest I've been in a very long time, and it shows in those pictures. Whether it is him or another man or woman or friend, it shouldn't matter. What should matter is that I am happy and living my life.

What I heard from you is you're not happy with my choice. That is fine. You said you wouldn't lose me over it either. I would hope not. However, the tone of your voice speaks differently. You additionally said you would not partake in helping me financially if I continue in this choice and that I need to make a decision. To me that last line is not the same as above. You won't lose me, but you will threaten me with money or lack thereof if I continue to see this man? An ultimatum.

I will be ok with being broke or going in debt. Money is not all that matters to me. Yes it sure helps, but my happiness is most important to me. Regardless if it is him or another person, White, Black or Hispanic. I'm not going to be bullied or controlled because you don't like my choices. Whatever they may be. And that is exactly what you did. I feel like I'm in a movie based in the '50s and my dad is dictating who I may and may not see. But it's not the '50s. I'm not 18. This isn't a movie.

I do not want to lose you. You are my dad. I love you more than anything besides my girls and this whole thing is killing me. I just got out of a controlling marriage to go to a controlling parent? I'm not good at ultimatums. Not since the new me has come out. I have grown so much as a person this last year. It has been amazing. It has been an excellent journey. I'm not even close to the person I was a year ago. I am strong. I see things differently. I view people differently. I make decisions in my life and my girls lives differently. It is a great thing. I am free. I am happy and I love myself. It is amazing.

I will never leave your life. I would never leave your life. None of this is truly about me or on me. It's about you. What you don't like. So actually the choice is yours not mine. I'm not owning any of the actions you choose to make. They are all yours. I hope you choose love over hate and all that goes with it.

I hope you choose me over hate and the color of a person. I hope you choose me over what other people think. Believe it or not the world is not as small minded as you think it is. I will not lose my job. My life is not in a ditch as you say. It's actually good. My life is great. My girls are great. My work is great. My friends are *great. Not one person is disowning me or ending a friendship.*

I'm going to live my life the way I want it. Not to please or accommodate others so much I lose myself, my wants and desires and my happiness in the process.

I will be waiting to hear from you. Take your time. I love you.

I waited for a response. I sent that at 10:00 am. His response came at 4:30pm.

All I have ever wanted was you to be happy. I'm glad you are and hope it continues.

I didn't know what to say. I sent him a text 6 weeks later because I did not want to go without talking to him any longer. We would text on and off. He told me once it hurt more to talk to me than not. I didn't quite understand that. I saw him later that year when my cousin passed away. It was awkward. I am writing this today and I have not heard from him since my birthday in November 2018. It's now January 2020. It's been more than a year. My girls have gone to see him a few times but it is extremely awkward to all of us. Any birthday cards or Christmas stuff that the girls get, my dad sends to my ex-husband's house instead of mine. My dad and ex-husband still communicate with each other via text or email. Which I find incredibly insane. I tell my dad I am leaving my ex and he tells me it's about damn time. Now they appear to be friends. Wow!

What have I taken from this? I have been given an incredible man that adds so much to my life. This situation with my dad made me realize how controlled I was by my father. As I look back, I think of conversations where my dad was manipulating me with money by setting all these rules. But later when we discussed it, he would recall the details differently than they actually were presented. I had walked on eggshells with my dad and my ex for so many years trying not to ruffle their feathers or have my kids ruffle their feathers. In hindsight, I wasn't living at all when I was around them. I was living to please them. I always made sure my dad was staying somewhere comfortable and to his liking. He got what he wanted when he wanted. I made sure the girls didn't act up or do something he didn't condone. Looking back, it was too much, it stressed me at a massive level.

I am choosing me. I am choosing Charles and my girls. I am choosing to have people in my life that want the best for us, not them. Every experience I have come to face, since the day I left, has been healing. My dad and this book included. It hurts all the time and it still hurts deeply that it was that easy for my dad to turn away from me and not have a relationship with me anymore. However, through the tears that it inevitably caused, I see love, hope, joy, freedom and my best life. I have left that door open for my Dad to reach out to me. I will welcome it. I loved him and I will still love him. I'm no longer the person that I once was though. No matter what, this time I will choose me. I have to choose me. I am strong enough to choose me and I will continue to choose me.

CHAPTER 11

BATTLE

SCARS

Wounds heal. Scars can last a lifetime.

– Cami Martin

Emotional and verbal abuse has deep wounds. They leave deep emotional scars. They heal, but some take longer than others. Some scars may never go away. I am healing, I have a lot of healing left to do though. The healing comes at some the craziest moments and it will continue to happen as life goes on. Charles has helped me with this, but he didn't know it was going to happen on this day. This past spring we were needing to get some things done around his house. He was under a time crunch. Charles needed to mow and weed eat the grass. Both would be hard to do separately and have them done in time. I told him I could mow. I wouldn't mind. He asked, "Are you sure, do you really want to mow?" "Yes," I said. "I don't mind at all." I thought to myself, "When was the last time that I mowed a yard." I mowed once or twice when I was married but only those couple of times. I wasn't "allowed" to mow at our house anymore. I mowed when I was in high school all the time. Today I wanted to mow. I welcomed it. It sounded like it would be fun and I would be helping Charles at the same time. So, I got the mower and I started mowing. As I mowed that day, I experienced many emotions. One was excitement, "Woohoo I was mowing!" The other was "Wow, I don't know the last time I really mowed" then "I hope I don't mess up" the next, "I hope I don't run over anything" followed by, "I hope I don't break something" then came, "Oh gosh what if I break something" after that, "Oh no, what if I do mess up something," finally the tears started flowing.

What I went through were emotions that had to do with messing up or breaking something. All of those feelings and emotions had to do with my past. In my past relationship I was always made to feel like I did things wrong daily. When those things were done wrong according to him, I was yelled at, then told I couldn't do it. I was told I didn't know how to do it right then I was made to feel stupid, inferior and beaten down verbally. As I was mowing, running over sticks, probably not mowing in a straight line and missing spots, Charles walked over to bring me a drink of water and said, "Take a drink baby." Wow. What is this? I'm not sure how to react to this type of kindness. He continued with, "Are you OK? Do you need a break? Do you want some more water?" I looked at him with tears running down my cheeks, I smiled and said,

"Thank you, I'm doing good" then smiled bigger. "Baby, what is wrong?" he asks again. I tell him, "I have had a trigger while I was mowing but I am ok. It's good. I will tell you more when we are done".

As I continued to mow the tears started falling again. The emotions overtook me as I realized no one was going to tell me I was doing it wrong. I didn't need to worry that I was going to break something. I wasn't going to be yelled at, called an idiot or have any of those comments. That part of my life was over and behind me. Charles had finished weed eating and walked back over to me to give me a break. I was definitely ok with taking a break and talking to him. He asked me again, "What happened babe?" I answered by explaining how I got afraid that I was going to break the lawnmower. I thought I might accidentally run over something or mow something wrong. It reminded me that I always got yelled at about those things. The flashback of it all scared me and I started crying because I didn't know mowing was another trigger. After Charles realized what had happened, he told me, "Baby, if you broke it, we would just go buy another one. It is a lawnmower, it doesn't matter. If you didn't mow it straight, it doesn't matter. Most of the lawn got mowed. Those are things that just don't matter. I would never get mad or upset with you about things like that." Again, tears because I knew he was different. I knew he would never do any of those things. I loved hearing how it was just a lawnmower and we could buy another one. It was the best afternoon of healing. I didn't realize how deep that wound was or that I even would feel that way. It was a therapy session. It was a healing session and it was a moment that freed me from my past. I will mow again and it's ok if I break it! We will buy another one!

As if mowing the lawn was not enough, let's paint too! The next weekend we painted! "Hahaha! Painting!!!! OMG! Can I handle this?" I thought seriously, are you kidding me. This was more daunting! It's paint and it will get everywhere. It has to be perfect! My mind was going crazy! He sees my face as he brings the rollers and paint out. There must have been a bit of anxiety on my face as he says, "We are painting, it doesn't have to be perfect. It is just paint. OK?" I looked at the roller, the paint and thought, "Oh hell!" I don't know about this. I heard what he was saying but my brain wasn't thinking the same thing. My brain thought don't drip the paint, don't get it on anything that it's not supposed to be on. Here we go again I thought with a chuckle. You got this! I was so afraid of dripping paint on the floor, being sloppy, really making a mess and not painting to someone else's expectations. I am staring at the roller. My mind going in circles. Then I hear this chuckle from him, and then "Oh no, nope, not today. No therapy today for you!" he says as he laughs. He senses my anxiety without me even speaking it out loud. He knows what I am thinking and he does something absolutely crazy! He takes the brush, dips it in the paint can then proceeds to drip it all over the floor. Next, he smashed it all over the wall getting it on everything and making a complete mess. His actions made me laugh so much that all those feelings and concerns left immediately. I just looked at him and smiled that big smile then I kissed him and I said, "Thank you, you are absolutely amazing!" Wow, what a feeling! Did he really just do that? Yes, he did! We painted the whole hallway. The floor had paint all over it, my feet had paint on them. The roller was messy, the doorknobs got paint on them and life felt beautiful the whole entire time. We enjoyed a great day together with no stress, no worry just lots of laughter and smiles. It was a perfect moment and an imperfect paint job. It was an amazing afternoon.

I went to bed that night smiling. Smiling so big I couldn't fall asleep. I had a full on, all teeth showing, giant heart felt smile. That smile turned into a laugh. He already knew why I was laughing and laughed with me. I felt grateful, blessed, happy and full of joy. My life, yes this is my life. Life can be good to you! Choose YOU!

CHAPTER 12

CHOOSING

ME

Sometimes the bad things that happen in our lives put us directly on the path to the best things that will ever happen to us.

— Nicole Reed

Is everyday fantastic? No! Do I learn something every day? No, but almost. My goal is to make the most out of each day, to take in all the good things, to filter out the negative and to be the type of person who chooses to "stop and smell the roses" every single day. As I sit in my kitchen right now to type, I look around me in amazement of how far I have come. It has been 3 years since I left. My life is so different now. I went from an apartment to a house. I have the backyard of my dreams with a sanctuary full of flowers, outdoor furniture and an outdoor fireplace. I actually have two outdoor spaces now; the second one has a hot tub. My entire adult life I have dreamed of an outdoor space like this one. My own personal haven. I have it now and I love it. It helps me think, it helps me relax and it helps me feel. It is an amazing space.

Every day I feel blessed. I am grateful. The gratitude I have flows through me as I desire to share it with the world! I have traveled and experienced more new things in the last three years, than I have done in the last 30 years of my life. I have been enjoying places I have wanted to visit for years. This has been the most fulfilling 3 years of my life. I have been choosing things

I like and want to experience. These had been adventures we both have wanted to experience. What an amazing adventure it has been for us. Surviving this storm has turned me into a very thankful person. I know what it is like to not be able to choose myself or things I desire and want. For decades, I was denied the right to pick the destinations I went to and the activities I did. I know what it is like to be beaten down by words. I now know what it is like to be loved and lifted up. I know I love myself and where to find love inside myself as well as when to allow others in. Learning to let people in was a giant step. Learning to feel and to be vulnerable. When you have been hurt your whole life, it makes you want to shut everyone out and never feel again. It makes you afraid of who will hurt you next. You become determined not let it happen again. We have all said it at some point in our lives, "No one will hurt me again!" However, if you aren't open to feeling love and vulnerability, then you are not open to anything including yourself.

I decided to find myself, to know myself and to truly embrace myself. When I was able to love me for who I was, for all my quirks and all the different things about me that make me who I am, I was able to open up even more. I was able to feel free, to be real, to be genuine and to be transparent. This happened when I chose to let all my guards down. When I wasn't going to be afraid of being hurt. It occurred when I decided I wasn't going to block out key people in my life who just wanted to love me. That is when I was able to show love, give love and receive love. I was able to show everyone the real me that had been locked away for so long. By doing this I became 100% okay with the person I now saw in the mirror. To look at her and smile. You got this! You got the world in the palm of your hand and life is about to be an amazing adventure!

CHAPTER 13

THE

STAGE

Be bold enough to use your voice, brave
enough to listen to your heart, and strong
enough to live the life you've always imagined.
- Unknown

The light is bright in my face, almost blinding. The microphone is all but a blur, and I hardly know it exists in front of me. What does exist in front of me is a crowd of people. They are sitting, watching and waiting to hear what I am about to say. *Who is this woman?* they must be thinking. *What is her story?* The theme for the night is *Inspire*. I wanted this moment to stop in time. I wanted to look at their faces. Hear all the sounds, look at the lights and the whole room. It was my first time telling my story in front of people. It was the moment I was realizing my dream. Finally, it had come, and I took in every single moment of it.

Throughout most of the prior ten years, I'd known I wanted to be a speaker. I can go through journals and see that dream written multiple times throughout many years. Tonight was the night it was all coming true. I was nervous and hoping I wasn't going to mess up. My biggest hope was that I would inspire someone. That they would hear my story and feel empowered. They would realize they were not alone. I wanted to inspire them to keep moving forward.

I have dreamed about this night multiple times. What the venue would look like? How many people would be in attendance? Would I be nervous? What I would wear? How my hair would look. What jewelry I would choose? I had envisioned it all and now, it was finally happening. My dream was about to come true.

I went shopping the day before the event. I wanted to find that special outfit. I found a one-piece black pant suit. It was perfect, except it wasn't long enough. Pants are never long enough, but there was enough hem to be altered! Ha! How in the world would I get it altered though? I was scheduled to speak tomorrow! I called around and found someone to alter it. They could let it out and have it ready by three o'clock on the day of the event. Fantastic! I dropped it off and made sure she understood I had to have it by 3:00 at the latest. She did, gave me a smile and said, "I will see you tomorrow!"

The time came and I went and picked it up. My fingers were crossed it was ready. I didn't try it on I just thanked her profusely and headed home to start getting ready. My makeup was done, my hair was just finished, all is going perfectly. I put the outfit on. Hmm? That feels kind of weird on that one leg. What is going on? Oh my gosh! The outside leg hadn't been sewn back together! They didn't sew the leg back together after they let out the hem. What! Ok. Ok. It's ok. I think to myself actually it will be ok and I can pull it off. It almost looks like it is supposed to be that way. It looks like a slit on one side of my leg. It will work! I won't tell anyone! Oh, my gosh!

The day is April 6, 2018. I am beyond excited to be part of an event put together by one of my friends, Bee Smith with BeeInspired. We were all going to be inspired by four featured speakers. I kept going over what I was going to say while I finished getting ready. It will be totally fine I kept telling myself. *Put your shoes on, girl! It will be great.* Let's go!

I'd been preparing for weeks for this but really, I had been preparing my whole life. I knew this day would come. The outfit, the accessories, the speech, it was all happening now. I am about to tell the audience about my journey. I could recite it in my sleep, but there were so many amazing details I kept going over it, I wanted to make sure I left nothing out.

Charles arrived at my apartment early. He could see the nerves mounting. As he drove us to the venue the nerves continued. I was sweating!

We arrived early so we could see the venue and meet the other speakers and the emcee for the night. It was set up very nicely. There were 17 tables that sat 6 people. The tables were covered with black tablecloths and each table had beautiful centerpieces. I saw a buffet of food that the guest would filter through prior to us speaking. There were big, bright lights set up to showcase the speakers and video cameras as well as sound equipment all in their spots This was going to be big! Lots of people were expected. Charles and I went to the green room where we met the other speakers. We all got to talk and share stories and relax a little before it all got started. I was very happy to have this time to breathe. I needed this chance to calm my nerves. My stomach was doing some backflips.

It was time to go find our seats. We walked through the seating area, to the tables reserved up front for the speakers and their families or guests to sit. Charles and I found our spot. I looked over the room. There were probably going to be about a hundred people here. Oh my goodness. *"Breathe."* I hear whispered in my ear. There was an agenda on the table with the speakers listed. At that moment I saw my name. *I am a speaker*. This was really happening!

"Breathe." Again, I heard it being whispered in my ear. I can feel my heart rate increasing as my time to speak got closer. We go through the buffet and eat before the speakers are called to come up. We got acquainted with all of the people at our table. I kept looking over my notes. I felt the nerves increase more. *"Breathe. You got this."* There was that whisper again. The calming voice that makes me smile when I hear it. That whisper was Charles. His voice telling me to breathe. He could feel the nerves. The heart rate increased. Every time he felt me get anxious, I heard him say *"Breathe."* Each time he told me to breathe, I would take a breath, smile and feel his words calm me.

Bee walked to the podium. She addressed everyone and thanked them for coming. Holy cow. It is getting close. *"Breathe."*

The first speaker came up, then the next. Wow, they are both great and talked about amazing experiences in their lives. I started to think, "I hope I can do as well as they did. I hope everyone claps when I'm finished. I hope they all enjoy it." Will they clap?

Oh my, it's my turn. Oh damn, I am about to be introduced. Oh my gosh, I have to walk to the podium and tell everyone my story. Tell everyone about me. My journey. *"Breathe. You are going to be amazing."*

I smiled at Charles, then I stand. I walked to the front of the room. I stood in front of the clear podium. It had a microphone and a place to put my notes. I laid them down. I stood there and made eye contact with every single person in that room. I smiled big. I said, "I am standing here in a moment of realization for me and I want to take it all in. This is a moment I have waited for, for a very long time. I want to take it all in, every detail. I want to see you and feel you and fully experience this moment I have dreamed about." My eyes welled up with tears. I looked at Bee and said, "Thank you."

Everyone was smiling back at me. The light was bright in front of me, as I start talking, the audience slowly fades from my focus. I forget about the microphone and I forget about the podium. I told them about myself, my "I have been 6'2 since birth" line. They laughed. I talked about my childhood, the marriage to my abusive ex-husband.

193

My nerves are now completely gone, I am not having to use any notes. I continued with my stories and told everyone about my reset trip. I then told them all my favorite part of the reset trip, when I said, "Watch me, watch me become a speaker!"

I then said, "Tonight I stand before you and I am a speaker. I am a giver of joy, positivity and inspiration."

I was living my dream at that exact moment. I felt so strong, confident, and special. Tears streamed down my face. Then the moment I was hoping for but wasn't sure what it would be like. They clapped, but what they did next made the tears flow even more. They stood up! I received a standing ovation. I could not believe it. I wanted to pinch myself.

I will never forget that night, it will be etched in my brain for eternity. The venue, the tables, the food, the pictures, the whole night. It was perfect.

As the event concluded, people flooded the front to thank me for telling my story and being so courageous and strong. Many expressed to me that they had lived a similar story or had a family member that was in an identical situation. I managed to smile with giant tears of gratitude as I continued to live this surreal moment.

It was a perfect night. That was the moment I knew I was doing what I had been called to do for the first time in my life. I knew this was my work. This was my passion. This was my dream come true. I will speak. I will share. I will inspire. I will keep moving forward and help others do the same.

CHAPTER 14

WATCH

ME!

Follow your heart and never let anyone take your dreams away. – John Assaaf

Watch me! Watch me choose me! Six words that defined a moment in time that would be life changing. Six words that were so empowering they still, to this day, resonate like nothing I had ever said in my life. Six words that mean strength, power and self-love. Six words that set me free. Six words that helped me reach my dream of speaking.

I hope you get the same feelings I get from those words. I hope you hear them and they empower you to choose you. I hope they empower you to know you are stronger than you think. They should remind you that can face any of the obstacles in front of you. Let these words empower you to control your life and your future.

I am not ashamed of my story or my journey. I am not ashamed to stand up in front of hundreds or thousands of people around the world. My story will heal, inspire and help someone know they can get through whatever they may be facing.

I want to help others claim their truth and walk away from their fears. I want you to stop caring so much what other people think so you can start caring about yourself and what you think. I have worried about others wants, thought and desires for so long concerned more about how it would affect them over how it would affect me. Your mind, your body, your spirit comes before others.

What I learned these last 3 years...

I am a work in progress, always.
I am a fighter and a dreamer.
I am capable of all the things my heart desires.
I am a giver and an inspirer.
I am the most positive person you will meet that has faced the giants that I have faced in my life.
I am living without fear.
I am full of joy, energy, positivity, life and happiness.
I am grateful for my trials, tribulations, successes, growth and all the people I have in my life.
I am building a legacy to empower YOU!
And...
I am beautiful
I am powerful

I am strong

And….

I am choosing me…

WATCH ME CHOOSE ME!